MW01223932

The Bridge of the Gods A Romance of Indian Oregon. 19th Edition.

by Balch, Frederic Homer, 1861-1891

ISBN: 9781318966493

Ordering Information:

Quantity sales. Special discounts are available on quantity purchases by corporations, associations, and others. For details, contact the publisher by email at the address above.

Printed in the United States of America, United Kingdom and Australia

THE BRIDGE OF THE GODS

"What think you now, Tohomish?"

THE BRIDGE

OF THE GODS

A Romance of Indian Oregon

By F. H. BALCH

With eight full-page illustrations by

L. MAYNARD DIXON

NINETEENTH EDITION

CHICAGO . A. C. McCLURG & CO.

NINETEEN HUNDRED & FIFTEEN

W. F. HALL PRINTING COMPANY, CHICAGO

PUBLISHERS' NOTE

Encouraged by the steady demand for Mr. Balch's "The Bridge of the Gods," since its publication twelve years ago, the publishers have decided to issue a new edition beautified with drawings from the pencil of Mr. L. Maynard Dixon. This tale of the Indians of the far West has fairly earned its lasting popularity, not only by the intense interest of the story, but by its faithful delineations of Indian character.

In his boyhood Mr. Balch enjoyed exceptional opportunities to inform himself regarding the character and manners of the Indians: he visited them in their homes, watched their industries, heard their legends, saw their gambling games, listened to their conversation; he questioned the Indians and the white pioneers, and he read many books for information on Indian history, traditions, and legends. By personal inquiry among old natives he learned that the Bridge which suggested the title of his romance was no fabric of the imagination, but was a great natural bridge that in early days spanned the Columbia, and later, according to tradition, was destroyed by an earthquake.

Before his death the author had the satisfaction of knowing that his work was stamped with the approval of the press and the public; his satisfaction would have been more complete could he have foreseen that that approval would be so lasting.

JULY 1, 1902.

PREFACE.

In attempting to present with romantic setting a truthful and realistic picture of the powerful and picturesque Indian tribes that inhabited the Oregon country two centuries ago, the author could not be indifferent to the many serious difficulties inseparable from such an enterprise. Of the literary success with which his work has been accomplished, he must of course leave others to judge; but he may without immodesty speak briefly of his preparation for his task, and of the foundation of some of the facts and legends which form the framework of his story. Indian life and character have long been a favorite study with him, and in these pages he has attempted to describe them, not from an ideal standpoint, but as he knew them in his own boyhood on the Upper Columbia. Many of the incidents related in the story have come under his personal observation; others have been told him by aged pioneers, or gleaned from old books of Northwestern travel. The every-day life of the Indians, their food, their dress, their methods of making their mats, of building their houses, of shaping their canoes, their gambling games, their religious beliefs, their legends, their subjects of conversation, the sports and pastimes of their children,—all these have been studied at first hand, and with the advantages of familiar and friendly intercourse with these people in their own homes. By constant questioning, many facts viii have been gained regarding their ancestry, and the fragments of history, tradition, and legend that have come down from them. Indian antiquities have been studied through every available source of information. All the antiquarian collections in Oregon and California have been consulted, old trading-posts visited, and old pioneers and early missionaries conversed with. Nothing has been discarded as trivial or insignificant that could aid in the slightest degree in affording an insight into Indian character and customs of a by-gone age.

As to the great Confederacy of the Wauna, it may be said that Gray's "History of Oregon" tells us of an alliance of several tribes on the Upper Columbia for mutual protection and defence; and students of Northwestern history will recall the great confederacy that the Yakima war-chief Kamyakin formed against the whites in the war of 1856, when the Indian tribes were in revolt from the British Possessions to the California line. Signal-fires announcing war against the whites leaped from hill to hill, flashing out in the night, till the line of fire beginning at the wild Okanogan ended a thousand miles south, on the foot-hills of Mount Shasta. Knowing such a confederacy as this to be an historical fact, there seems nothing improbable in that part of the legend which tells us that in ancient times the Indian tribes on either side of the Cascade Range united under the great war-chief Multnomah against their hereditary foes the Shoshones. Even this would not be so extensive a confederacy as that which Kamyakin formed a hundred and fifty years later.

It may be asked if there was ever a great natural bridge over the Columbia,—a "Bridge of the Gods," such as the legend describes. The answer is emphatically, "Yes." Everywhere along the mid-Columbia the Indians tell of a great bridge that once spanned the river where the cascades now are, but where at that time the placid ix current flowed under an arch of stone; that this bridge was *tomanowos*, built by the gods; that the Great Spirit shook the earth, and the bridge crashed down into the river, forming the present obstruction of the cascades. All of the Columbian tribes tell this story, in different versions and in different dialects, but all agreeing upon its essential features as one of the great facts of their past history.

"*Ancutta* (long time back)," say the Tumwater Indians, "the salmon he no pass Tumwater falls. It too much big leap. Snake Indian he no catch um fish above falls. By and by great *tomanowos* bridge at cascades he fall in, dam up water, make river higher all way up to Tumwater; then salmon he get over. Then Snake Indian all time catch um plenty."

"My father talk one time," said an old Klickitat to a pioneer at White Salmon, Washington; "long time ago liddle boy, him in canoe, his mother paddle, paddle up Columbia, then come to *tomanowos* bridge. Squaw paddle canoe under; all dark under bridge. He look up, all like one big roof, shut out sky, no see um sun. Indian afraid, paddle quick, get past soon, no good. Liddle boy no forget how bridge look."

Local proof also is not wanting. In the fall, when the freshets are over and the waters of the Columbia are clear, one going out in a small boat just above the cascades and looking down into the transparent depths can see submerged forest trees beneath him, still standing upright as they stood before the bridge fell in and the river was raised above them. It is a strange, weird sight, this forest beneath the river; the waters wash over the broken tree-tops, fish swim among the leafless branches: it is desolate, spectre-like, beyond all words. Scientific men who have examined the field with a view to determining the credibility of the legend about the bridge are convinced that it is essentially true. Believed in by many x tribes, attested by the appearance of the locality, and confirmed by geological investigation, it is surely entitled to be received as a historic fact.

The shipwreck of an Oriental vessel on the Oregon coast, which furnishes one of the most romantic elements in our story, is an altogether probable historic incident, as explained more fully in a foot-note on page 75.

The spelling of Indian names, in which authorities differ so widely, has been made as accurate as possible; and, as in the name "Wallulah," the oldest and most Indian-like form has been chosen. An exception has been made in the case of the modernized and corrupted "Willamette," which is used instead of the original Indian name, "Wallamet." But the meaningless "Willamette" has unfortunately passed into such general use that one is almost compelled to accept it. Another verbal irregularity should be noticed: Wauna, the name given by all the Indians in the story to the Columbia, was only the Klickitat name for it. The Indians had no general name for the Columbia, but each tribe had a special name, if any, for it. Some had no name for it at all. It was simply "the big water," "*the* river," "the big salmon water." What Wauna, the Klickitat name, or Wemath, the Wasco name, signifies, the author has been unable to learn, even from the Indians who gave him the names. They do not know; they say their fathers knew, but it is forgotten now.

A rich and splendid treasure of legend and lore has passed away with the old pioneers and the Indians of the earlier generation. All that may be found interesting in this or any other book on the Indians, compared to what has been lost, is like "a torn leaf from some old romance."

F. H. B.

OAKLAND, CALIFORNIA,
September, 1890.

CONTENTS.

Book I.

THE APOSTLE TO THE INDIANS.

Book II.

THE OPENING OF THE DRAMA.

Book III.

THE GATHERING OF THE TRIBES.

𝔅ook IV. xii

THE LOVE TALE.

Book V.

THE SHADOW OF THE END.

ILLUSTRATIONS.

Multnomah's Death-
canoe

*Facing
page* 264

What tall and tawny men were these,
As sombre, silent, as the trees
They moved among! and sad some way
With tempered sadness, ever they,
Yet not with sorrow born of fear,
The shadows of their destinies
They saw approaching year by year,
And murmured not.

    ·   ·   ·   ·   ·

They turned to death as to a sleep,
And died with eager hands held out
To reaching hands beyond the deep;
And died with choicest bow at hand,
And quiver full and arrow drawn
For use, when sweet to-morrow's dawn
Should wake them in the Spirit Land.

JOAQUIN MILLER.

THE BRIDGE OF THE GODS.

BOOK I.

THE APOSTLE TO THE INDIANS.

CHAPTER I.

THE NEW ENGLAND MEETING.

Such as sit in darkness and the shadow of death.—
Bible.

One Sabbath morning more than two hundred years ago, the dawn broke clear and beautiful over New England. It was one of those lovely mornings that seem like a benediction, a smile of God upon the earth, so calm are they, so full of unutterable rest and quiet. Over the sea, with its endless line of beach and promontory washed softly by the ocean swells; over the towns of the coast,—Boston and Salem,—already large, giving splendid promise of the future; over the farms and hamlets of the interior, and into the rude clearings where the outer limits of civilization mingled with the primeval forest, came a flood of light as the sun rose above the blue line of eastern sea. And still beyond, across the Alleghanies, into the depth of the wilderness, passed the sweet, calm radiance, as if bearing a gleam of gospel sunshine to the Indians of the forest.

14

Nowhere did the Sunday seem more peaceful than in a sheltered valley in Massachusetts. Beautiful indeed were the thrifty orchards, the rustic farmhouses, the meadows where the charred stumps that marked the last clearing were festooned with running vines, the fields green with Indian corn, and around all the sweep of hills dark with the ancient wood. Even the grim unpainted meeting-house on the hill, which was wont to look the very personification of the rigid Calvinistic theology preached within it, seemed a little less bare and forbidding on that sweet June Sabbath.

As the hour for morning service drew near, the drummer took his accustomed stand before the church and began to thunder forth his summons,—a summons not unfitting those stern Puritans whose idea of religion was that of a life-long warfare against the world, the flesh, and the devil.

Soon the people began to gather,—grave men and women, dressed in the sober-colored garb of the day, and little children, clad in their "Sunday best," undergoing the awful process of "going to meeting," yet some of them, at least, looking at the cool shadowed wood as they passed, and thinking how pleasant it would be to hunt berries or birds' nests in those sylvan retreats instead of listening to a two hours' sermon, under imminent danger of perdition if they went to sleep,—for in such seductive guise did the Evil One tempt the souls of these youthful Puritans. Solemn of visage and garb were the groups, although here and there the gleam of a bit of ribbon at the throat of some young maiden, or a bonnet tastefully adorned, showed that "the world, the flesh, and 15 the devil" were not yet wholly subdued among them.

As the audience filed through the open door, the men and women divided, the former taking one side of the house, the latter the other,—the aisle forming a dividing line between them. The floor was uncarpeted, the walls bare, the pulpit undraped, and upon it the hour-glass stood beside the open Bible. Anything more stiff and barren than the interior of the meeting-house it would be difficult to find.

An unwonted stir breaks the silence and solemnity of the waiting congregation, as an official party enters. It is the Governor of the colony and his staff, who are making a tour of the province, and have stopped over Sunday in the little frontier settlement,—for although the Governor is an august man, even he may not presume to travel on the Sabbath in this land of the Puritans. The new-comers are richly dressed. There is something heavy, massive, and splendid in their garb, especially in the Governor's. He is a stately military-looking man, and wears his ample vestments, his embroidered gloves, his lace and ruffles, with a magisterial air.

A rustle goes through the audience as the distinguished visitors pass up the aisle to the front seats assigned, as the custom was, to dignitaries. Young people steal curious glances at them; children turn around in their seats to stare, provoking divers shakes of the head from their elders, and in one instance the boxing of an ear, at which the culprit sets up a smothered howl, is ignominiously shaken, and sits swelling and choking with indignant grief during the remainder of the service.

16

At length the drum ceased, indicating both the arrival of the minister and the time for service to begin.

The minister took his place in the pulpit. He was a young man, of delicate mould, with a pale and intellectual face. Exquisite sensitiveness was in the large gray eyes, the white brow, the delicate lips, the long slender fingers; yet will and energy and command were in them all. His was that rare union of extreme sensibility with strong resolution that has given the world its religious leaders,—its Savonarolas and Chrysostoms; men whose nerves shrank at a discord in music, but when inspired by some grand cause, were like steel to suffer and endure.

Something of this was in the minister's aspect, as he stood before the people that morning. His eyes shone and dilated, and his slight figure gathered dignity as his gaze met that of the assembly. There was no organ, that instrument being deemed a device of the Prince of Darkness to lead the hearts of the unwary off to popery; but the opening hymn was heartily sung. Then came the Scripture reading,—usually a very monotonous performance on the part of Puritan divines; but as given in the young minister's thoughtfully modulated voice, nothing could have been more expressive. Every word had its meaning, every metaphor was a picture; the whole psalm seemed to breathe with life and power: "Lord, thou hast been our dwelling-place in all generations."

Majestic, mournful, yet thrilling with deathless hope, was the minister's voice; and the people were deeply moved. The prayer followed,—not the endless 17 monologue of the average Puritan clergyman, but pointed, significant, full of meaning. Again his face was lifted before them as he rose to announce the text. It was paler now; the eyes were glowing and luminous; the long, expressive fingers were tremulous with excitement. It was evident to all that no common subject was to be introduced, no common effort to be made. Always composed, the audience grew more quiet still. The very children felt the hush of expectation, and gazed wonderingly at the minister. Even that great man, the Governor, lost his air of unbending grandeur, and leaned expectantly forward.

The subject was Paul's vision of the man in Macedonia crying for help. The speaker portrayed in burning words the condition of Macedonia, the heathen gloom and utter hopelessness of her people, the vision that came to Paul, and his going to preach to them. Then, passing to England under the Druids, he described the dark paganism, the blood-stained altars, the brutal priesthood of the age; and told of the cry that went forth for light,—a cry that touched the heart of the Roman Gregory into sending missionaries to show them the better way.

Like some royal poem was the discourse, as it showed how, through the storms and perils of more than a thousand years, amid the persecution of popes, the wars of barons, and the tyranny of kings, England had kept the torch burning, till in these latter times it had filled the world with light. Beautiful was the tribute he paid to the more recent defenders of the faith, and most intense the interest of the listeners; for men sat there who had come over the seas because of their loyalty to the faith,—old and grizzled 18 men, whose youth had known Cromwell and Charles Stuart, and who had in more recent years fought for "King Monmouth" and shared the dark fortunes of Argyle.

The old Governor was roused like a veteran war-horse at the sound of the trumpet; many faces were flushed with martial ardor. The young minister paused reflectively at the enthusiasm he had kindled. A sorrowful smile flitted around his lips, though the glow of inspiration was still burning in his eyes. Would they be as enthusiastic when he made the application of his discourse?

And yet England, yea, even New England, was false, disloyal. She had but half kept the faith. When the cry of pagan England had gone forth for light, it had been heard; the light had been given. But now in her day of illumination, when the Macedonian cry came to her, she closed her ears and listened not. On her skirts was the blood of the souls of men; and at the last day the wail of the heathen as they went down into the gulf of flame would bear witness against her.

Grave and impassioned, with an undertone of warning and sorrow, rang the voice of the minister, and the hearts of the people were shaken as though a prophet were speaking.

"Out from the forests around us come the cry of heathen folk, and ye will not listen. Ye have the light, and they perish in darkness and go down to the pit. Generation after generation has grown up here in forest and mountain, and has lived and died without God and without hope. Generation has followed generation, stumbling blindly downward to the 19 dust like the brutes that perish. And now their children, bound in iron and sitting under the shadow of death, reach out their hands from the wilderness with a blind cry to you for help. Will ye hear?"

He lifted his hands to them as he spoke; there was infinite pathos in his voice; for a moment it seemed as if all the wild people of the wilderness were pleading through him for light. Tears were in many eyes; yet in spite of the wonderful power of his oratory, there were faces that grew stern as he spoke,—for only a few years had passed since the Pequod war, and the feeling against the Indians was bitter. The Governor now sat erect and indignant.

Strong and vehement was the minister's plea for missionaries to be sent to the Indians; fearlessly was the colonial government arraigned for its deficiencies in this regard; and the sands in the hour-glass were almost run out when the sermon was concluded and the minister sank flushed and exhausted into his seat.

The closing psalm was sung, and the audience was dismissed. Slow and lingering were the words of the benediction, as if the preacher were conscious of defeat and longed to plead still further with his people. Then the gathering broke up, the congregation filing out with the same solemnity that had marked the entrance. But when the open air was reached, the pent-up excitement burst forth in a general murmur of comment.

"A good man," remarked the Governor to his staff, "but young, quite young." And they smiled approvingly at the grim irony of the tone.

"Our pastor is a fine speaker," said another, "but 20 why will he bring such unpleasant things into the pulpit? A good doctrinal sermon, now, would have strengthened our faith and edified us all."

"Ay, a sermon on the errors of Episcopacy, for instance."

"Such talk makes me angry," growled a third. "Missionaries for the Indians! when the bones of the good folk they have killed are yet bleaching amid the ashes of their cabins! Missionaries for those red demons! an' had it been powder and shot for them it had been a righteous sermon."

So the murmur of disapprobation went on among those slowly dispersing groups who dreaded and hated the Indian with an intensity such as we now can hardly realize. And among them came the minister, pale and downcast, realizing that he had dashed himself in vain against the stern prejudice of his people and his age.

21

CHAPTER II.

THE MINISTER'S HOME.

Sore have I panted at the sun's decline,
To pass with him into the crimson West,
And see the peoples of the evening.

EDWIN ARNOLD.

The Reverend Cecil Grey,—for such was our young minister's name,—proceeded immediately after the service to his home. Before we cross its threshold with him, let us pause for a moment to look back over his past life.

Born in New England, he first received from his father, who was a fine scholar, a careful home training, and was then sent to England to complete his education. At Magdalen College, Oxford, he spent six years. Time passed very happily with him in the quiet cloisters of that most beautiful of English colleges, with its memories of Pole and Rupert, and the more courtly traditions of the state that Richard and Edward had held there. But when, in 1687, James II. attempted to trample on the privileges of the Fellows and force upon them a popish president, Cecil was one of those who made the famous protest against it; and when protests availed nothing, he left Oxford, as also did a number of others. Returning to America, he was appointed pastor of a New England church, becoming one of the many who carried the 22 flower of scholarship and eloquence into the bleak wilds of the New World.

Restless, sensitive, ardent, he was a man to whom a settled pastorate was impossible. Daring enterprises, great undertakings of a religious nature yet full of peril, were the things for which he was naturally fitted; and amid the monotonous routine of parish duties he longed for a greater activity. Two centuries later he might have become distinguished as a revivalist or as a champion of new and startling views of theology; earlier, he might have been a reformer, a follower of Luther or Loyola; as it was, he was out of his sphere.

But for a time the Reverend Mr. Grey tried hard to mould himself to his new work. He went with anxious fidelity through all the labors of the country pastorate. He visited and prayed with the sick, he read the Bible to the old and dim-sighted, he tried to reconcile petty quarrels, he wrestled with his own discontent, and strove hard to grind down all the aspirations of his nature and shut out the larger horizon of life.

And for a time he was successful; but during it he was induced to take a very fatal step. He was young, handsome, a clergyman, and unmarried. Now a young unmarried minister is pre-eminently one of sorrows and acquainted with grief. For that large body of well-meaning people who are by nature incapacitated from attending to their own business take him in hand without mercy. Innumerable are the ways in which he is informed that he ought to be married. Subtle and past finding out are the plots laid by all the old ladies and match-makers of his church to 23 promote that desired event. He is told that he can never succeed in the ministry till he is married. The praises of Matilda Jane Tompkins or Lucinda Brown are sounded in his ears till he almost wishes that both were in a better world,—a world more worthy their virtues. At length, wearily capitulating, he marries some wooden-faced or angular saint, and is unhappy for life.

Now there was in Mr. Grey's church a good, gentle girl, narrow but not wooden-faced, famous for her neatness and her housekeeping abilities, who was supposed to be the pattern for a minister's wife. In time gone by she had set her heart on a graceless sailor lad who was drowned at sea, much to the relief of her parents. Ruth Anderson had mourned for him quietly, shutting up her sorrow in her own breast and going about her work as before; for hers was one of those subdued, practical natures that seek relief from trouble in hard work.

She seemed in the judgment of all the old women in the church the "very one" for Mr. Grey; and it likewise seemed that Mr. Grey was the "very one" for her. So divers hints were dropped and divers things were said, until each began to wonder if marriage were not a duty. The Reverend Cecil Grey began to take unusual pains with his toilet, and wended his way up the hill to Mr. Anderson's with very much the aspect of a man who is going to be hanged. And his attempts at conversation with the maiden were not at all what might have been expected from the young minister whose graceful presence and fluent eloquence had been the boast of Magdalen. On her part the embarrassment was equally great. At length they 24 were married,—a marriage based on a false idea of duty on each side. But no idea of duty, however strong or however false, could blind the eyes of this married pair to the terrible fact that not only love but mental sympathy was wanting. Day by day Cecil felt that his wife did not love him, that her thoughts were not for him, that it was an effort for her to act the part of a wife toward him. Day by day she felt that his interests lay beyond her reach, and that all the tenderness in his manner toward her came from a sense of duty, not from love.

But she strove in all ways to be a faithful wife, and he tried hard to be a kind and devoted husband. He had been especially attentive to her of late, for her health had been failing, and the old doctor had shaken his head very gravely over her. For a week or more she had grown steadily worse, and was now unable even to walk without help. Her malady was one of those that sap away the life with a swift and deadly power against which all human skill seems unavailing.

Mr. Grey on returning from church entered the living room. The invalid sat at the window, a heavy shawl wrapped about her, her pale face turned to the far blue line of sea, visible through a gap in the hills. A pang wrenched his heart keenly at the sight. Why *would* she always sit at that window looking so sorrowfully, so abstractedly at the sea, as if her heart was buried there with her dead lover?

She started as she heard his footstep, and turned her head quickly toward him, a faint flush tinging her cheek and a forced smile quivering around her lips. Her greeting was very gentle, and he saw that her 25 heart was reproaching her for being so disloyal to him as to think of her lost lover; and yet he felt her fingers tremble and shrink away from his as he took her hand.

"God forgive me!" he thought, with infinite self-accusation. "How repugnant I must be to her,—an intruder, thrusting myself into the heart that is sacred to the dead."

But he let her see nothing of this in his voice or manner as he inquired how she had been. She replied wearily that she was no better, that she longed to get well again and be at work.

"I missed your sermon to-day," she said, with that strained, pathetic smile upon her lips again. "You must tell me about it now."

He drew his chair to her side and began to give an outline of the sermon. She listened, but it was with forced attention, without sympathy, without in the least entering into the spirit of what he was saying. It pained him. He knew that her nature was so narrow, so conventional, that it was impossible for her to comprehend his grand scheme of Indian evangelization. But he checked his impatience, and gave her a full synopsis of the discourse.

"It is useless, useless. They cannot understand. A whole race is perishing around them, and they will not put forth a hand save to mistreat a Quaker or throw a stone at a Churchman. Our Puritanism is like iron to resist tyranny,—but alas! it is like iron, too, when one tries to bend it to some generous undertaking."

He stopped, checking back other and more bitter words. All his soul rose up in revolt against the prejudice 26 by which he was surrounded. Then Ruth spoke timidly.

"Seeing that it is so, would it not be best to let this missionary subject go, and preach on practical every-day matters? I am not wise in these things, I know; but would it not be better to preach on common subjects, showing us how we ought to live from day to day, than to discourse of those larger things that the people do not understand?"

His face darkened, though not angrily. This was the same prejudice he had just encountered in the meeting-house, though in a different form. He arose and paced back and forth with quick, impatient steps.

Then he came and stood before her with folded arms and resolute face.

"Ruth, I have tried that so often, tried it with prayers and tears, but it is utterly impossible. I cannot bring myself to it. You know what the physicians say of my disease of the heart,—that my life may be very short; and I want it to be noble. I want to live for the greatest possibilities within my reach. I want to set some great work in motion that will light up thousands of darkened lives,—yea, and grow in might and power even after my lips are sealed in death."

The little figure on the chair moved uneasily under his animated though kindly gaze.

"I do not quite comprehend you. I think the best work is to do what God gives us to do, and to do it well. To me he has given to labor in caring for the house,"—there was a patient weariness in her tone that did not escape Cecil,—"to you he has given the duties of a pastor, to strengthen the weak, cheer the sorrowing, 27 comfort the old. Is it not better to do those things faithfully than to spend our time longing for some more ideal work not given us?"

"But suppose the ideal work is given? Suppose a man is called to proclaim new truths, and be the leader in a new reform? For him the quiet pastorate is impossible; nay, were it possible, it would be wrong, for would he not be keeping back the message God had given him? He would be one called to a work, yet entering not upon it; and upon him would come the curse that fell on the unfaithful prophets of old."

All the gloom of the theology of his age was on him as he spoke. Refined and poetic as was his nature, it was thoroughly imbued with the Calvinism of early New England.

She lifted her hand wearily and passed it over her aching brow.

"I do not know," she said; "I have never thought of such things, only it seems to me that God knew best when he gave us our lots in life. Surely wherever we find ourselves, there he intended us to be, and there we should patiently work, leaving our higher aspirations to his will. Is not the ideal life, after all, the one that is kindest and humblest?"

"But, Ruth," replied the minister, sadly, "while the work you describe is certainly noble, I have yet felt for a long time that it is not what God calls me to. Day after day, night after night, I think of the wild races that roam the forests to the west, of which no man knows the end. Sometimes I think that I am called to stand before the rulers of the colony and plead that missionaries be sent to the Indians. 28 Sometimes I feel that I am called to go and preach to them myself. Often in my dreams I plead with dark-browed sachems or with mighty gatherings of warriors to cast away their blood-stained weapons and accept Christ, till I awake all trembling with the effort. And always the deadly pain at my heart warns me that what is done must be done quickly."

The burning ardor that had given such intensity to his sermon came into his voice as he spoke. The invalid moved nervously on her chair, and he saw that his enthusiasm merely jarred on her without awakening any response.

"Forgive me," he said hurriedly, "I forgot that you were not well enough to talk of those things. Sometime when you are better we will speak of them again."

And then he talked of other and to her more interesting topics, while a keen pang rankled in his breast to find her irresponsive to that which was so dear to him.

But he was very kind to her; and when after a while the old Indian woman, Cecil's nurse in childhood and their only servant now, came to tell him that dinner was ready, he would not go until he had first brought his wife her dinner and waited on her with his own hands.

After his own repast was finished he must hasten away to preach his afternoon sermon. But he came to her first and bent over her; for though love never had been, perhaps never could be, between them, there was a deep domestic feeling in his nature.

"How good and patient you are in your sickness," he said, gazing down into the quiet, wistful face that 29 was so honest and true, yet so thoroughly prosaic and commonplace. "What a sermon you have been preaching me, sitting here so uncomplainingly."

"Do you think so?" she said, looking up gratefully. "I am glad. I so want to do my duty by you."

He had meant to kiss her as he bent over her, though such caresses were rare between them, but there was something in her tones that chilled him, and he merely raised a tress of her hair to his lips instead. At the door he bade her a pleasant farewell, but his countenance grew sorrowful as he went down the path.

"Duty," he murmured, "always duty, never love. Well, the fault is my own that we were ever married. God help me to be true and kind to her always. She shall never know that I miss anything in her."

And he preached to his congregation that afternoon a sermon on burden-bearing, showing how each should bear his own burden patiently,—not darkening the lives of others by complaint, but always saying loving words, no matter how much of heartache lay beneath them. He told how near God is to us all, ready to heal and to strengthen; and closed by showing how sweet and beautiful even a common life may grow through brave and self-sacrificing endurance of trouble.

It was a helpful sermon, a sermon that brought the listeners nearer God. More than one heart was touched by those earnest words that seemed to breathe divine sympathy and compassion.

He went home feeling more at peace than he had done for many days. His wife's room was still, as he 30 entered it. She was in her easy-chair at the window, lying back among the pillows asleep. Her face was flushed and feverish, her long lashes wet with tears. The wraps had fallen away from her, and he stooped over to replace them. As he did so her lips moved in her half-delirious slumber, and she murmured some name sounding like his own. A wild throb of joy thrilled through him, and he bent closer to listen. Again she spoke the name, spoke it sorrowfully, longingly. It was the name of her lover drowned at sea.

The long, nervous fingers that held the half-drawn wraps shook convulsively as with acutest pain, then drew the coverings gently around her.

"God help her, God help her!" he murmured, as he turned softly away, his eyes filling with tears,—tears for her sorrow rather than his own.

31

CHAPTER III.

A DARKENED FIRESIDE.

... Her way is parted from my way;
Out of sight, beyond light, at what goal may we
meet?

DANTE ROSSETTI.

Ruth was much worse in the evening, but at last, after Cecil had watched at her side till a late hour, she sank into a troubled sleep. Then the old Indian servant insisted on taking his place at the sufferer's bedside, for she saw that he was much worn by the labors of the day and by anxiety for his wife. At first he refused; but she was a skilled nurse, and he knew that the invalid would fare better in her hands than his own, so at last he consented on condition that she would call him if his wife grew worse. The woman promised, and he withdrew into the library, where a temporary bed had been made for him. At the door he turned and looked back.

His wife lay with closed eyes and flushed face amid the white pillows. The robe over her breast stirred with her difficult breathing, and her head turned now and then from side to side while she uttered broken, feverish words. By her sat the swarthy nurse, watching her every movement and ready with observant eye and gentle touch to minister to all her needs.

A yearning tenderness and pity came into his gaze. "Poor child, poor child!" he thought. "If I could only make her well and happy! If I could only bring 32 her dead lover back to life, how gladly would I put her in his arms and go away forever!" And it seemed to him in some dim way that he had wronged the poor sufferer; that he was to blame for her sorrow.

He went on into the library. A lamp was burning on the table; a Hebrew Bible and a copy of Homer lay beside it. Along the walls were arranged those heavy and ponderous tomes in which the theology of the age was wont to clothe itself.

He seated himself at the table and took up his Homer; for he was too agitated to sleep. But it was in vain that he tried to interest himself in it. The rhythm had lost its music, the thought its power; it was in vain that he tried to forget himself in the reply of Achilles, or the struggle over the body of Patroclus.

Hawthorne tells us that a person of artistic temperament may at a time of mental depression wander through the Roman galleries and see nothing in the finest masterpieces of Raphael or Angelo. The grace is gone from the picture, the inspiration from the marble; the one is a meaningless collection of colors, the other a dull effigy carved in stone.

Something of this mood was on Cecil to-night. Irresponsive to the grand beauty of the poem he felt only its undertone of heartache and woe.

"It is like human life," he thought, as he listlessly turned the pages; "it is bright on the surface, but dark and terrible with pain below. What a black mystery is life! what bitter irony of justice! Hector is dragged at Achilles' chariot-wheel, and Paris goes free. Helen returns to her home in triumph, while 33 Andromache is left desolate. Did Homer write in satire, and is the Iliad but a splendid mockery of justice, human and divine? Or is life so sad that every tale woven of it must needs become a tragedy?"

He pondered the gloomy puzzle of human existence long that night. At length his brain grew over-weary, and he slept sitting in his chair, his head resting on the pages of the open book.

How long he slept he knew not, but he awoke with a start to find a hand laid on his shoulder and the tall figure of the Indian woman standing beside him. He sprang up in sudden fear.

"Is she worse?" he cried. But the woman, with that light noiseless step, that mute stolidity so characteristic of her race, had already glided to the door; and there was no need for her to answer, for already his own apprehensions had replied.

He was in the room almost as soon as she. His wife was much worse; and hastening through the night to a neighboring farmhouse, he roused its inmates, despatched a messenger for the physician, and returned, accompanied by several members of the neighbor's family.

The slow moments dragged away like years as they watched around her. It seemed as if the doctor would never come. To the end of his life Cecil never forgot the long-drawn agony of that night.

At length their strained hearing caught the quick tread of horses' hoofs on the turf without.

"The doctor, the doctor!" came simultaneously from the lips of Cecil and the watchers. The doctor,—there was hope in the very name.

How eagerly they watched his face as he bent over 34 the patient! It was a calm, self-contained face, but they saw a shadow flit over it, a sudden almost imperceptible change of expression that said "Death" as plainly as if he had spoken it. They could do nothing, he said,—nothing but wait for the end to come.

How the moments lingered! Sometimes Cecil bent over the sufferer with every muscle quivering to her paroxysms; sometimes he could endure it no longer and went out into the cool night air or into the library, where with the mere mechanical instinct of a student he picked up a book, reading a few lines in it, then throwing it aside. Yet wherever he was he felt her sufferings as acutely as when standing by her side. His whole frame was in keenest sympathy with hers, his whole being full of pain. So sharp were his sensations that they imparted an abnormal vigor to his mind. Every line his eyes met in reading stood out on the page with wonderful distinctness. The words seemed pictorial, and his mind grasped abstruse propositions or involved expressions with marvellous facility.

He noted it, and remembered afterward that he thought at the time how curious it was that his tortured sympathies should give him such startling acuteness of perception.

The slow night waned, the slow dawn crept over the eastern hills. Cecil stood with haggard eyes at the foot of the bed, watching the sleeper's face. As the daylight brightened, blending with the light of the still burning lamps, he saw a change come over her countenance; the set face relaxed, the look lost its wildness. A great hope shone in his hollow eyes.

"She is getting better, she is coming out of her sufferings," he whispered to the doctor.

35

"She will be out of her sufferings very soon," he replied sadly; and then Cecil knew that the end was at hand. Was it because the peace, the profound serenity which sometimes is the prelude of death, filling her being, penetrated his, that he grew so strangely calm? An inexpressible solemnity came to him as he looked at her, and all his agitation left him.

Her face grew very sweet and calm, and full of peace. Her eyes met Cecil's, and there was in them something that seemed to thank him for all his goodness and patience,—something that was both benediction and farewell. Her lips moved, but she was past the power of speech, and only her eyes thanked him in a tender, grateful glance.

The sun's edge flashed above the horizon, and its first rays fell through the uncurtained window full upon her face. She turned toward them, smiling faintly, and her face grew tenderly, radiantly beautiful, as if on that beam of sunshine the spirit of her dead lover had come to greet her from the sea. Then the sparkle died out of her eyes and the smile faded from her lips. It was only a white, dead face that lay there bathed in golden light.

A moment after, Cecil left the house with swift footsteps and plunged into the adjacent wood. There under a spreading oak he flung himself prone upon the earth, and buried his face in his hands. A seething turmoil of thoughts swept his mind. The past rose before him like a panorama. All his married life rushed back upon him, and every memory was regret and accusation.

"I might have been kinder to her, I might have been better," he murmured, while the hot tears gushed 36 from his eyes. "I might have been so much better to her," he repeated over and over,—he, whose whole thought had been to shut up his sorrow in his own heart and show her only tenderness and consideration.

By and by he grew calmer and sat up, leaning against the tree and looking out into vacancy with dim eyes that saw nothing. His heart was desolate, emptied of everything. What was he to do? What was he to set before himself? He had not loved her, but still she had been a part of his life; with what was he to fill it now?

As he sat there depressed and troubled, a strange thing happened.

He was looking, as has been said, blindly into vacancy. It may have been an optical illusion, it may have been a mere vagary born of an over-wrought brain; but a picture formed before him. In the distance, toward the west, he saw something that looked like a great arch of stone, a natural bridge, rugged with crags and dark with pine. Beneath it swept a wide blue river, and on it wild horsemen were crossing and recrossing, with plumed hair and rude lances. Their faces were Indian, yet of a type different from any he had ever seen. The bridge was in the heart of a mighty mountain-range. On either side rose sharp and lofty peaks, their sides worn by the action of water in some remote age.

These details he noted as in a dream; then the strangeness of it all burst upon him. Even as it did so, the vision dissolved; the bridge wavered and passed away, the mountain-peaks sank in shadow. He leaped to his feet and gazed eagerly. A fine mist seemed passing before his sight; then he saw only the reach 37 of hill and woodland, with the morning light resting upon it.

While the vision faded, he felt springing up within him an irrepressible desire to follow it. A mysterious fascination seized him, a wild desire to seek the phantom bridge. His whole being was swayed as by a supernatural power toward the west whence the vision had passed. He started forward eagerly, then checked himself in bewilderment. What could it mean?

In the nineteenth century, one similarly affected would think it meant a fevered, a disordered brain; but in the seventeenth, when statesmen like Cromwell believed in dreams and omens, and *roués* like Monmouth carried charms in their pockets, these things were differently regarded.

The Puritan ministry, whose minds were imbued with the gloomy supernaturalism of the Old Testament on which they fed, were especially men to whom anything resembling an apparition had a prophetic significance. And Cecil Grey, though liberal beyond most New England clergymen, was liable by the keenness of his susceptibilities and the extreme sensitiveness of his organization to be influenced by such delusions,—if delusions they be. So he stood awed and trembling, questioning within himself, like some seer to whom a dark and uncertain revelation has been made.

Suddenly the answer came.

"The Lord hath revealed his will unto me and shown me the path wherein I am to walk," he murmured in a hushed and stricken tone. "Ruth was taken from me that I might be free to go where he should send me. The vision of the Indians and the 38 bridge which faded into the west, and the strange desire that was given me to follow it, show that the Lord has another work for me to do. And when I find the land of the bridge and of the wild people I saw upon it, then will I find the mission that God has given me to do. 'Lord God of Israel, I thank Thee. Thou hast shown me the way, and I will walk in it, though all its stones be fire and its end be death.'"

He stood a moment with bowed head, communing with his God. Then he returned to his lonely home.

The friends whose kindly sympathies had brought them to the house of mourning wondered at the erect carriage, the rapt, exalted manner of the man. His face was pale, almost as pale as that within the darkened room; but his eyes shone, and his lips were closely, resolutely set.

A little while, and that determined face was all sorrowful and pitying again, as he bent over the still, cold body of his dead.

39

CHAPTER IV.

THE COUNCIL OF ORDINATION.

Friends were assembled together; the Elder and Magistrate   also
Graced the scene with their presence, and stood like the   Law   and
the   Gospel....
After the Puritan way and the laudable custom of Holland.

The Courtship of Miles Standish.

A few days after the funeral, letters missive from the little society went out to all the neighboring churches, calling a council to ordain the Reverend Cecil Grey a missionary to the Indians.

It was a novel thing, in spite of the noble example that Roger Williams had set not many years before; and the summons met with a general response.

All the churches, far and near, sent delegates. If one could only have taken a peep, the day before the council, into the households of that part of New England, what a glimpse he would have gotten of Puritan domestic life! What a brushing up there was of black coats, what a careful starching and ironing of bands; and above all, in Cecil's own neighborhood, what a mighty cookery for the ordination dinner the next day! For verily the capacity of the clerical stomach is marvellous, and is in fact the one thing in theology that does not change. New departures alter doctrines, creeds are modified, but the appetite of the clergy is not subject to such mutations.

40

The morrow came, and with it the expected guests. The meeting house was crowded. There were many ministers and lay delegates in the council. In the chair sat a venerable preacher, not unknown in the records of those days,—a portly man, with a shrewd and kindly face. Sterner faces were there also. The council wore a grave aspect, more like a court of judges before whom a criminal is cited to appear than an assembly of clergymen about to ordain a missionary.

After some preliminaries, Cecil was called on to give a statement of his reasons for wishing to go as an evangelist to the Indians. He rose before them. There was a singular contrast between his slight form and expressive features and the stout frames and grim countenances of the others. But the graceful presence of the man had in it a quiet dignity that commanded the respect of all.

In obedience to the command, he told how he had thought of the unknown tribes beyond the Alleghanies, living in the gloom of paganism and perishing in darkness, till an intangible sympathy inclined him toward them,—till, as it seemed to him, their great desire for light had entered into and possessed him, drawing him toward them by a mysterious and irresistible attraction. He felt called of God to go and minister to their spiritual needs, and that it was his duty to leave everything and obey the call.

"Is this all?" he was asked.

He hesitated a moment, and then described his vision in the wood the morning of his wife's death. It made a deep impression on his hearers. There was scarcely a man in the assembly who was not tinged with the superstition of the age; and all listened, not lightly or sceptically, but in awe, as if it brought them to the threshold of the supernatural.

When the narration was ended, the chairman requested him to retire, pending the decision of the council; but first he was asked,—

"Are you willing to abide by the decision of this council, whatever it may be?"

He raised his head confidently, and his reply came frank and fearless.

"I shall respect the opinions of my brethren, no matter how they may decide; but I shall abide by the will of God and my own convictions of duty."

The grave Puritan bent his head, half in acknowledgment of the reply, half in involuntary admiration of its brave manhood; then Cecil left the room, the silent, watchful crowd that filled the aisles parting respectfully to let him pass.

"Now, brethren," said the chairman, "the matter is before you. Let us hear from each his judgment upon it."

Solemn and weighty were the opinions delivered. One brother thought that Mr. Grey had plenty of work to do at home without going off on a wild-goose chase after the heathen folk of the wilderness. His church needed him; to leave it thus would be a shameful neglect of duty.

Another thought that the Indians were descendants of the ten lost tribes of Israel, and as such should be left in the hands of God. To attempt to evangelize them was to fly in the face of Providence.

Another thought the same; but then, how about 42 that vision of Mr. Grey? He couldn't get around that vision.

"I don't know, brethren, I don't know!" he concluded, shaking his head.

Still another declared positively for Mr. Grey. The good people of the colonies owed it to the savages to do something for their religious enlightenment. It was wrong that so little had been done. They had taken their land from them, they had pushed them back into the wilds at the point of the sword; now let them try to save their souls. This man had been plainly called of God to be an apostle to the Indians; the least that they could do was to bid him Godspeed and let him go.

So it went on. At length the venerable chairman, who had twice turned the hour-glass upon the table before him, rose to close the discussion. His speech was a singular mixture of shrewdness, benevolence, and superstition.

He said that, as Christians, they certainly owed a duty to the Indians,—a duty that had not been performed. Mr. Grey wished to help fulfil that neglected obligation, and would go at his own expense. It would not cost the church a shilling. His vision was certainly a revelation of the will of the Lord, and *he* dared not stand in the way.

A vote was taken, and the majority were found to be in favor of ordination. The chairman pronounced himself pleased, and Mr. Grey was recalled and informed of the result.

"I thank you," he said simply, with a glad and grateful smile.

"Now, brethren," said the worthy chairman with 43 much unction, "the hour of dinner is nigh at hand, and the good people of this place have prepared entertainment for us; so we will e'en put off the ceremony of ordination till the afternoon. Let us look to the Lord for his blessing, and be dismissed."

And so with a murmur of talk and comment the council broke up, its members going to the places where they were to be entertained. Happy was the man who returned to his home accompanied by a minister, while those not so fortunate were fain to be content with a lay delegate. Indeed, the hospitality of the settlement was so bounteous that the supply exceeded the demand. There were not enough visitors to go around; and more than one good housewife who had baked, boiled, and roasted all the day before was moved to righteous indignation at the sight of the good man of the house returning guestless from the meeting.

Early in the afternoon entertainers and entertained gathered again at the meeting-house. Almost the entire country side was there,—old and young alike. The house was packed, for never before had that part of New England seen a man ordained to carry the gospel to the Indians. It occurred, too, in that dreary interval between the persecution of the Quakers and the persecution of the witches, and was therefore doubly welcome.

When Cecil arrived, the throng made way reverently for him. Was he not going, perchance like the martyrs of old, to the fagot and the stake? To those who had long known him he seemed hardly like the same man. He was lifted to a higher plane, surrounded by an atmosphere of sanctity and heroism, 44 and made sacred by the high mission given him of God, to which was now to be added the sanction of holy men.

So they made way for him, as the Florentines had made way for "il Frate" and as the people of God had made way for Francis Xavier when he left them to stir the heart of the East with his eloquence, and, alas! to die on the bleak sea-coast of China, clasping the crucifix to his breast and praying for those who had cast him out.

Cecil's face, though pale, was calm and noble. All his nature responded to the moral grandeur of the occasion. It would be difficult to put into words the reverent and tender exaltation of feeling that animated him that day. Perhaps only those upon whose own heads the hands of ordination have been laid can enter into or understand it.

The charge was earnest, but it was not needed, for Cecil's ardent enthusiasm went far beyond all that the speaker urged upon him. As he listened, pausing as it were on the threshold of an unknown future, he wondered if he should ever hear a sermon again,—he, so soon to be swallowed by darkness, swept, self-yielded, into the abyss of savagery.

Heartfelt and touching was the prayer of ordination,—that God might accept and bless Cecil's consecration, that the divine presence might always abide with him, that savage hearts might be touched and softened, that savage lives might be lighted up through his instrumentality, and that seed might be sown in the wilderness which would spring up and cause the waste places to be glad and the desert to blossom as the rose.

45

"And so," said the old minister, his voice faltering and his hands trembling as they rested on Cecil's bowed head, "so we give him into Thine own hand and send him forth into the wilderness. Thou only knowest what is before him, whether it be a harvest of souls, or torture and death. But we know that, for the Christian, persecutions and trials are but stepping-stones leading to God; yea, and that death itself is victory. And if he is faithful, we know that whatever his lot may be it will be glorious; that whatever the end may be, it will be but a door opening into the presence of the Most High."

Strong and triumphant rang the old man's tones, as he closed his prayer committing Cecil into the hands of God. To him, as he listened, it seemed as if the last tie that bound him to New England was severed, and he stood consecrated and anointed for his mission. When he raised his face, more than one of the onlookers thought of those words of the Book where it speaks of Stephen,—"And they saw his face as it had been the face of an angel."

A psalm was sung, the benediction given, and the solemn service was over. It was long, however, before the people left the house. They lingered around Cecil, bidding him farewell, for he was to go forth at dawn the next day upon his mission. They pressed his hand, some with warm words of sympathy, some silently and with wet eyes. Many affectionate words were said, for they had never known before how much they loved their pastor; and now he seemed no longer a pastor, but a martyr and a saint. More than one mother brought him her child to bless;—others strangers from a distance— lifted their children 46 up, so that they could see him above the press, while they whispered to them that they must always remember that they had seen the good Mr. Grey, who was going far off into the west to tell the Indians about God.

Long afterward, when nearly all that generation had passed away and the storm of the Revolution was beginning to gather over the colonies, there were a few aged men still living who sometimes told how, when they were children, they had seen Cecil Grey bidding the people farewell at the old meeting-house; and through all the lapse of years they remembered what a wonderful brightness was on his face, and how sweet and kind were his words to each as he bade them good-by forever.

47

CHAPTER V.

INTO TRACKLESS WILDS.

"I will depart," he said, "the hour is come,
And in the silence of yon sky I read
My   fated   message   flashing."

EDWIN ARNOLD.

The next morning Cecil rose early after a sleepless night. On that day he was to go out from all that was sweet and precious in life and take the path into the wilderness. At first his heart sank within him; then his strength of purpose revived, and he was resolute again.

He must go, and soon. The briefer the parting the briefer the pang. He had already bidden his friends good-by; his parents were long since dead; it only remained to part from the old Indian woman, his nurse in childhood, now his faithful housekeeper and the only inmate of his home.

He went to the kitchen,—for usually at this hour she was up and preparing breakfast. She was not there, and the room looked cold and cheerless in the gray dawn. He went to her door and knocked; there was no response. He called her; the room was as still as death. Alarmed, he opened the door; no one was within; she was gone,— had evidently been gone all night, for the bed was untouched.

He was pained and bewildered at this desertion, for only the day before he had given her a paper 48 legally drawn up, securing to her the little property he possessed and making her independent for the rest of her life. She had taken it, listened in silence to the kindly expressions that accompanied the gift, and turned away without a word. Now she was gone; what could it mean?

Slowly he made the simple preparations that were needed for the journey—putting a little food, his Bible, and other necessaries into a kind of knapsack and strapping it upon his back. Then taking his staff, he went out from his home, never to return.

The sun was rising, the air was fresh and dewy, but his heart was sad. Yet through it ran a strange thrill of joy, a strange blending of pain and gladness.

"The parting is bitter, bitter almost unto death, but He will keep me," murmured the white lips, as he went down the walk.

The sound of voices fell on his ears, and he looked up. At the gate, awaiting him, was a group of his parishioners, who had come to look once more on the face of their pastor. One by whose bedside he had prayed in the hour of sickness; another, whom his counsel had saved when direly tempted; a little lame child, who loved him for his kindness; and an aged, dim-sighted woman, to whom he had often read the Scriptures.

He opened the gate and came out among them.

"God bless you, sir," said the old woman, "we wanted to see your bonny face again before you left us."

The little lame boy said nothing, but came up to Cecil, took his hand, and pressed it to his cheek in a manner more eloquent than words.

49

"Friends," said Cecil, in a faltering voice, "I thank you. It is very sweet to know that you care for me thus."

One by one they came and clasped his hand in tearful farewell. For each he had a loving word. It was an impressive scene,—the sorrow-stricken group, the pastor with his pale spiritual face full of calm resolve, and around them the solemn hush of morning.

When all had been spoken, the minister reverently uncovered his head; the others did the same. "It is for the last time," he said; "let us pray."

After a few earnest words commending them to the care of God, he drew his hand gently from the lame boy's cheek and rested it on his head in silent benediction. Then giving them one last look of unutterable love, a look they never forgot,—

"Good-by," he said softly, "God bless you all."

"Good-by, God bless *you*, sir," came back in answer; and they saw his face no more.

One more farewell was yet to be said. The winding path led close by the country graveyard. He entered it and knelt by the side of the new-made grave. Upon the wooden headboard was inscribed the name of her who slept beneath,—"Ruth Grey."

He kissed the cold sod, his tears falling fast upon it.

"Forgive me," he whispered, as if the dull ear of death could hear. "Forgive me for everything wherein I failed you. Forgive me, and— Farewell."

Again he was on his way. At the entrance to the wood he saw a figure sitting on a rock beside the path. As he drew nearer he observed it was clad in Indian garb, and evidently awaited his coming. Who 50 was it? Might it not be some chief, who, having heard of his intended mission, had come forth to meet him?

He hastened his steps. When he came nearer, he saw that it was only an Indian woman; a little closer, and to his inexpressible astonishment he recognized his old nurse.

"What does this mean?" he exclaimed. "What are you doing here, and in Indian garb, too?"

She rose to her feet with simple, natural dignity.

"It means," she said, "that I go with you. Was I not your nurse in childhood? Did I not carry you in my arms then, and has not your roof sheltered me since? Can I forsake him who is as my own child? My heart has twined around you too long to be torn away. Your path shall be my path; we go together."

It was in vain that Cecil protested, reasoned, argued.

"I have spoken," she said. "I will not turn back from my words while life is left me."

He would have pleaded longer, but she threw a light pack upon her back and went on into the forest. She had made her decision, and he knew she would adhere to it with the inflexible obstinacy of her race.

He could only follow her regretfully; and yet he could not but be grateful for her loyalty.

"I have spoken; I will not turn back from my words."

52

At the edge of the wood he paused and looked back. Before him lay the farms and orchards of the Puritans. Here and there a flock of sheep was being driven from the fold into the pasture, and a girl, bucket in hand, was taking her way to the milking shed. From each farmhouse a column of smoke rose into the clear air. Over all shone the glory of the morning sun. It was civilization; it was New England; it was *home*.

For a moment, the scene seemed literally to lay hold of him and pull him back. For a moment, all the domestic feelings, all the refinement in his nature, rose up in revolt against the rude contact with barbarism before him. It seemed as if he could not go on, as if he must go back. He shook like a leaf with the mighty conflict.

"My God!" he cried out, throwing up his arms with a despairing gesture, "must I give up everything, everything?"

He felt his resolution giving way; his gray eyes were dark and dilated with excitement and pain; his long fingers twitched and quivered; before he knew what he was doing, he was walking back toward the settlement.

That brought him to himself; that re-awakened the latent energy and decision of his character.

"What! shall I turn back from the very threshold of my work? God forgive me—never!"

His delicate frame grew strong and hardy under the power of his indomitable spirit. Again his dauntless enthusiasm came back; again he was the Apostle to the Indians.

One long last look, and he disappeared in the shadows of the wood, passing forever from the ken of the white man; for only vague rumors floated back to the colonies from those mysterious wilds into which he had plunged. The strange and wondrous tale of his after-life New England never knew.

BOOK II.

THE OPENING OF THE DRAMA.

CHAPTER I.

SHALL THE GREAT COUNCIL BE HELD?

The comet burns the wings of night,
And dazzles elements and spheres;
Then dies in beauty and a blaze of light
Blown far through other years.

JOAQUIN MILLER.

Two hundred years ago—as near as we can estimate the time from the dim and shadowy legends that have come down to us—the confederacy of the Wauna or Columbia was one of the most powerful the New World has ever seen. It was apparently not inferior to that of the Six Nations, or to the more transitory leagues with which Tecumseh or Pontiac stayed for a moment the onward march of the white man. It was a union of the Indian tribes of Oregon and Washington, with the Willamettes at the head, against their great hereditary enemies, the Nootkas, the Shoshones, and the Spokanes.

Sonorous and picturesque was the language of the old Oregon Indians in telling the first white traders the story of the great alliance.

54

"Once, long before my father's time and before his father's time, all the tribes were as one tribe and the Willamettes were *tyee* [chief]. The Willamettes were strong and none could stand against them. The heart of the Willamette was battle and his hand was blood. When he lifted his arm in war, his enemy's lodge became ashes and his council silence and death.

"The war-trails of the Willamette went north and south and east, and there was no grass on them. He called the Chinook and Sound Indians, who were weak, his children, and the Yakima, Cayuse, and Wasco, who loved war, his brothers; but *he* was elder brother. And the Spokanes and the Shoshones might fast and cut themselves with thorns and knives, and dance the medicine dance, and drink the blood of horses, but nothing could make their hearts as strong as the hearts of the Willamettes; for the One up in the sky had told the old men and the dreamers that the Willamettes should be the strongest of all the tribes as long as the Bridge of the Gods should stand. That was their *tomanowos*."

But whenever the white listener asked about this superstition of the bridge and the legend connected with it, the Indian would at once become uncommunicative, and say, "You can't understand," or more frequently, "I don't know." For the main difficulty in collecting these ancient tales—"old-man talk," as the Siwashes call them—was, that there was much superstition interwoven with them; and the Indians were so reticent about their religious beliefs, that if one was not exceedingly cautious, the lively, gesticulating talker of one moment was liable to become the personification of sullen obstinacy the next.

55

But if the listener was fortunate enough to strike the golden mean, being neither too anxious nor too indifferent, and if above all he had by the gift of bounteous *muck-a-muck* [food] touched the chord to which the savage heart always responds, the Indian might go on and tell in broken English or crude Chinook the strange, dark legend of the bridge, which is the subject of our tale.

At the time our story opens, this confederacy was at the height of its power. It was a rough-hewn, barbarian realm, the most heterogeneous, the most rudimentary of alliances. The exact manner of its union, its laws, its extent, and its origin are all involved in the darkness which everywhere covers the history of Indian Oregon,— a darkness into which our legend casts but a ray of light that makes the shadows seem the denser. It gives us, however, a glimpse of the diverse and squalid tribes that made up the confederacy. This included the "Canoe Indians" of the Sound and of the Oregon sea-coast, whose flat heads, greasy squat bodies, and crooked legs were in marked contrast with their skill and dexterity in managing their canoes and fish-spears; the hardy Indians of the Willamette Valley and the Cascade Range; and the bold, predatory riders of eastern Oregon and Washington,—buffalo hunters and horse tamers, passionately fond, long before the advent of the white man, of racing and gambling. It comprised also the Okanogans, who disposed of their dead by tying them upright to a tree; the Yakimas, who buried them under cairns of stone; the Klickitats, who swathed them like mummies and laid them in low, rude huts on the *mimaluse*, or "death islands" of 56 the Columbia; the Chinooks, who stretched them in canoes with paddles and fishing implements by their side; and the Kalamaths, who burned them with the maddest saturnalia of dancing, howling, and leaping through the flames of the funeral pyre. Over sixty or seventy petty tribes stretched the wild empire, welded together by the pressure of common foes and held in the grasp of the hereditary war-chief of the Willamettes.

The chiefs of the Willamettes had gathered on Wappatto Island, from time immemorial the council-ground of the tribes. The white man has changed its name to "Sauvie's" Island; but its wonderful beauty is unchangeable. Lying at the mouth of the Willamette River and extending for many miles down the Columbia, rich in wide meadows and crystal lakes, its interior dotted with majestic oaks and its shores fringed with cottonwoods, around it the blue and sweeping rivers, the wooded hills, and the far white snow peaks,—it is the most picturesque spot in Oregon.

The chiefs were assembled in secret council, and only those of pure Willamette blood were present, for the question to be considered was not one to be known by even the most trusted ally.

All the confederated tribes beyond the Cascade Range were in a ferment of rebellion. One of the petty tribes of eastern Oregon had recently risen up against the Willamette supremacy; and after a short but bloody struggle, the insurrection had been put down and the rebels almost exterminated by the victorious Willamettes.

57

But it was known that the chief of the malcontents had passed from tribe to tribe before the struggle commenced, inciting them to revolt, and it was suspected that a secret league had been formed; though when matters came to a crisis, the confederates, afraid to face openly the fierce warriors of the Willamette, had stood sullenly back, giving assistance to neither side. It was evident, however, that a spirit of angry discontent was rife among them. Threatening language had been used by the restless chiefs beyond the mountains; braves had talked around the camp-fire of the freedom of the days before the yoke of the confederacy was known; and the gray old dreamers, with whom the *mimaluse tillicums* [dead people] talked, had said that the fall of the Willamettes was near at hand.

The sachems of the Willamettes, advised of everything, were met in council in the soft Oregon spring-tide. They were gathered under the cottonwood trees, not far from the bank of the Columbia. The air was fresh with the scent of the waters, and the young leaves were just putting forth on the "trees of council," whose branches swayed gently in the breeze. Beneath them, their bronze faces more swarthy still as the dancing sunbeams fell upon them through the moving boughs, thirty sachems sat in close semi-circle before their great war-chief, Multnomah.

It was a strange, a sombre assembly. The chiefs were for the most part tall, well-built men, warriors and hunters from their youth up. There was something fierce and haughty in their bearing, something menacing, violent, and lawless in their saturnine faces and black, glittering eyes. Most of them wore their hair 58 long; some plaited, others flowing loosely over their shoulders. Their ears were loaded with *hiagua* shells; their dress was composed of buckskin leggings and moccasins, and a short robe of dressed skin that came from the shoulders to the knees, to which was added a kind of blanket woven of the wool of the mountain sheep, or an outer robe of skins or furs, stained various colors and always drawn close around the body when sitting or standing. Seated on rude mats of rushes, wrapped each in his outer blanket and doubly wrapped in Indian stoicism, the warriors were ranged before their chief.

His garb did not differ from that of the others, except that his blanket was of the richest fur known to the Indians, so doubled that the fur showed on either side. His bare arms were clasped each with a rough band of gold; his hair was cut short, in sign of mourning for his favorite wife, and his neck was adorned with a collar of large bear-claws, showing he had accomplished that proudest of all achievements for the Indian,—the killing of a grizzly.

Until the last chief had entered the grove and taken his place in the semi-circle, Multnomah sat like a statue of stone. He leaned forward reclining on his bow, a fine unstrung weapon tipped with gold. He was about sixty years old, his form tall and stately, his brow high, his eyes black, overhung with shaggy gray eyebrows and piercing as an eagle's. His dark, grandly impassive face, with its imposing regularity of feature, showed a penetration that read everything, a reserve that revealed nothing, a dominating power that gave strength and command to every line. The lip, the brow, the very grip of the hand on the bow 59 told of a despotic temper and an indomitable will. The glance that flashed out from this reserved and resolute face—sharp, searching, and imperious—may complete the portrait of Multnomah, the silent, the secret, the terrible.

When the last late-entering chief had taken his place, Multnomah rose and began to speak, using the royal language; for like the Cayuses and several other tribes of the Northwest, the Willamettes had two languages,—the common, for every-day use, and the royal, spoken only by the chiefs in council.

In grave, strong words he laid before them the troubles that threatened to break up the confederacy and his plan for meeting them. It was to send out runners calling a council of all the tribes, including the doubtful allies, and to try before them and execute the rebellious chief, who had been taken alive and was now reserved for the torture. Such a council, with the terrible warning of the rebel's death enacted before it, would awe the malcontents into submission or drive them into open revolt. Long enough had the allies spoken with two tongues; long enough had they smoked the peace-pipe with both the Willamettes and their enemies. They must come now to peace that should be peace, or to open war. The chief made no gestures, his voice did not vary its stern, deliberate accents from first to last; but there was an indefinable something in word and manner that told how his warlike soul thirsted for battle, how the iron resolution, the ferocity beneath his stoicism, burned with desire of vengeance.

There was perfect attention while he spoke,—not so much as a glance or a whisper aside. When he 60 had ceased and resumed his seat, silence reigned for a little while. Then Tla-wau-wau, chief of the Klackamas, a sub-tribe of the Willamette, rose. He laid aside his outer robe, leaving bare his arms and shoulders, which were deeply scarred; for Tla-wau-wau was a mighty warrior, and as such commanded. With measured deliberation he spoke in the royal tongue.

"Tla-wau-wau has seen many winters, and his hair is very gray. Many times has he watched the grass spring up and grow brown and wither, and the snows come and go, and those things have brought him wisdom, and what he has seen of life and death has given him strong thoughts. It is not well to leap headlong into a muddy stream, lest there be rocks under the black water. Shall we call the tribes to meet us here on the island of council? When they are all gathered together they are more numerous than we. Is it wise to call those that are stronger than ourselves into our wigwam, when their hearts are bitter against us? Who knows what plots they might lay, or how suddenly they might fall on us at night or in the day when we were unprepared? Can we trust them? Does not the Klickitat's name mean 'he that steals horses'? The Yakima would smoke the peace-pipe with the knife that was to stab you hid under his blanket. The Wasco's heart is a lie, and his tongue is a trap.

"No, let us wait. The tribes talk great swelling words now and their hearts are hot, but if we wait, the fire will die down and the words grow small. Then we can have a council and be knit together again. Let us wait till another winter has come and gone; then let us meet in council, and the tribes will listen.

61

"Tla-wau-wau says, 'wait, and all will be well.'"

His earnest, emphatic words ended, the chief took his seat and resumed his former look of stolid indifference. A moment before he had been all animation, every glance and gesture eloquent with meaning; now he sat seemingly impassive and unconcerned.

There was another pause. It was so still that the rustling of the boughs overhead was startlingly distinct. Saving the restless glitter of black eyes, it was a tableau of stoicism. Then another spoke, advising caution, setting forth the danger of plunging into a contest with the allies. Speaker followed speaker in the same strain.

As they uttered the words counselling delay, the glance of the war-chief grew ever brighter, and his grip upon the bow on which he leaned grew harder. But the cold face did not relax a muscle. At length rose Mishlah the Cougar, chief of the Mollalies. His was one of the most singular faces there. His tangled hair fell around a sinister, bestial countenance, all scarred and seamed by wounds received in battle. His head was almost flat, running back from his eyebrows so obliquely that when he stood erect he seemed to have no forehead at all; while the back and lower part of his head showed an enormous development,—a development that was all animal. He knew nothing but battle, and was one of the most dreaded warriors of the Willamettes.

He spoke,—not in the royal language, as did the others, but in the common dialect, the only one of which he was master.

"My heart is as the heart of Multnomah. Mishlah is hungry for war. If the tribes that are our younger 62 brothers are faithful, they will come to the council and smoke the pipe of peace with us; if they are not, let us know it. Mishlah knows not what it is to wait. You all talk words, words, words; and the tribes laugh and say, 'The Willamettes have become women and sit in the lodge sewing moccasins and are afraid to fight.' Send out the runners. Call the council. Let us find who are our enemies; then let us strike!"

The hands of the chief closed involuntarily as if they clutched a weapon, and his voice rang harsh and grating. The eyes of Multnomah flashed fire, and the war-lust kindled for a moment on the dark faces of the listeners.

Then rose the grotesque figure of an Indian, ancient, withered, with matted locks and haggard face, who had just joined the council, gliding in noiselessly from the neighboring wood. His cheek-bones were unusually high, his lower lip thick and protruding, his eyes deeply sunken, his face drawn, austere, and dismal beyond description. The mis-shapen, degraded features repelled at first sight; but a second glance revealed a great dim sadness in the eyes, a gloomy foreboding on brow and lip that were weirdly fascinating, so sombre were they, so full of woe. There was a wild dignity in his mien; and he wore the robe of furs, though soiled and torn, that only the richest chiefs were able to wear. Such was Tohomish, or Pine Voice, chief of the Santiam tribe of the Willamettes, the most eloquent orator and potent medicine or *tomanowos* man in the confederacy.

There was a perceptible movement of expectation, a lighting up of faces as he arose, and a shadow of 63 anxiety swept over Multnomah's impassive features. For this man's eloquence was wonderful, and his soft magnetic tones could sway the passions of his hearers to his will with a power that seemed more than human to the superstitious Indians. Would he declare for the council or against it; for peace or for war?

He threw back the tangled locks that hung over his face, and spoke.

"Chiefs and warriors, who dwell in lodges and talk with men, Tohomish, who dwells in caves and talks with the dead, says greeting, and by him the dead send greeting also."

His voice was wonderfully musical, thrilling, and pathetic; and as he spoke the salutation from the dead, a shudder went through the wild audience before him,—through all but Multnomah, who did not shrink nor drop his searching eyes from the speaker's face. What cared he for the salutation of the living or the dead? Would this man whose influence was so powerful declare for action or delay?

"It has been long since Tohomish has stood in the light of the sun and looked on the faces of his brothers or heard their voices. Other faces has he looked upon and other voices has he heard. He has learned the language of the birds and the trees, and has talked with the People of Old who dwell in the serpent and the cayote; and they have taught him their secrets. But of late terrible things have come to Tohomish."

He paused, and the silence was breathless, for the Indians looked on this man as a seer to whom the future was as luminous as the past. But Multnomah's brow darkened; he felt that Tohomish also 64 was against him, and the soul of the warrior rose up stern and resentful against the prophet.

"A few suns ago, as I wandered in the forest by the Santiam, I heard the death-wail in the distance. I said, 'Some one is dead, and that is the cry of the mourners. I will go and lift up my voice with them.' But as I sought them up the hill and through the thickets the cry grew fainter and farther, till at last it died out amid distant rocks and crags. And then I knew that I had heard no human voice lamenting the dead, but that it was the Spirit Indian-of-the-Wood wailing for the living whose feet go down to the darkness and whose faces the sun shall soon see no more. Then my heart grew heavy and bitter, for I knew that woe had come to the Willamettes.

"I went to my den in the mountains, and sought to know of those that dwell in the night the meaning of this. I built the medicine-fire, I fasted, I refused to sleep. Day and night I kept the fire burning; day and night I danced the *tomanowos* dance around the flames, or leaped through them, singing the song that brings the *Spee-ough*, till at last the life went from my limbs and my head grew sick and everything was a whirl of fire. Then I knew that the power was on me, and I fell, and all grew black.

"I dreamed a dream.

"I stood by the death-trail that leads to the spirit-land. The souls of those who had just died were passing; and as I gazed, the wail I had heard in the forest came back, but nearer than before. And as the wail sounded, the throng on the death-trail grew thicker and their tread swifter. The warrior passed with his bow in his hand and his quiver swinging from 65 his shoulder; the squaw followed with his food upon her back; the old tottered by. It was a whole people on the way to the spirit-land. But when I tried to see their faces, to know them, if they were Willamette or Shoshone or our brother tribes, I could not. But the wail grew ever louder and the dead grew ever thicker as they passed. Then it all faded out, and I slept. When I awoke, it was night; the fire had burned into ashes and the medicine wolf was howling on the hills. The voices that are in the air came to me and said, 'Go to the council and tell what you have seen;' but I refused, and went far into the wood to avoid them. But the voices would not let me rest, and my spirit burned within me, and I came. Beware of the great council. Send out no runners. Call not the tribes together. Voices and omens and dreams tell Tohomish of something terrible to come. The trees whisper it; it is in the air, in the waters. It has made my spirit bitter and heavy until my drink seems blood and my food has the taste of death. Warriors, Tohomish has shown his heart. His words are ended."

He resumed his seat and drew his robe about him, muffling the lower part of his face. The matted hair fell once more over his drooping brow and repulsive countenance, from which the light faded the moment he ceased to speak. Again the silence was profound. The Indians sat spell-bound, charmed by the mournful music of the prophet's voice and awed by the dread vision he had revealed. All the superstition within them was aroused. When Tohomish took his seat, every Indian was ready to oppose the calling of the council with all his might. Even Mishlah, as 66 superstitious as blood-thirsty, was startled and perplexed. The war-chief stood alone.

He knew it, but it only made his despotic will the stronger. Against the opposition of the council and the warning of Tohomish, against *tomanowos* and *Spee-ough*, ominous as they were even to him, rose up the instinct which was as much a part of him as life itself,—the instinct to battle and to conquer. He was resolved with all the grand strength of his nature to bend the council to his will, and with more than Indian subtility saw how it might be done.

He rose to his feet and stood for a moment in silence, sweeping with his glance the circle of chiefs. As he did so, the mere personality of the man began to produce a reaction. For forty years he had been the great war-chief of the tribes of the Wauna, and had never known defeat. The ancient enemies of his race dreaded him; the wandering bands of the prairies had carried his name far and wide; and even beyond the Rockies, Sioux and Pawnee had heard rumors of the powerful chief by the Big River of the West. He stood before them a huge, stern warrior, himself a living assurance of victory and dominion.

As was customary with Indian orators in preparing the way for a special appeal, he began to recount the deeds of the fathers, the valor of the ancient heroes of the race. His stoicism fell from him as he half spoke, half chanted the harangue. The passion that was burning within him made his words like pictures, so vivid they were, and thrilled his tones with electric power. As he went on, the sullen faces of his hearers grew animated; the superstitious fears that Tohomish had awakened fell from them. Again they were 67 warriors, and their blood kindled and their pulses throbbed to the words of their invincible leader. He saw it, and began to speak of the battles they themselves had fought and the victories they had gained. More than one dark cheek flushed darker and more than one hand moved unconsciously to the knife. He alluded to the recent war and to the rebellious tribe that had been destroyed.

"*That*," said he, "was the people Tohomish saw passing over the death-trail in his dream. What wonder that the thought of death should fill the air, when we have slain a whole people at a single blow! Do we not know too that their spirits would try to frighten our dreamers with omens and bad *tomanowos*? Was it not bad *tomanowos* that Tohomish saw? It could not have come from the Great Spirit, for he spoke to our fathers and said that we should be strongest of all the tribes as long as the Bridge of the Gods should stand. Have the stones of that bridge begun to crumble, that our hearts should grow weak?"

He then described the natural bridge which, as tradition and geology alike tell us, spanned at that time the Columbia at the Cascades. The Great Spirit, he declared, had spoken; and as he had said, so it would be. Dreams and omens were mist and shadow, but the bridge was rock, and the word of the Great Spirit stood forever. On this tradition the chief dwelt with tremendous force, setting against the superstition that Tohomish had roused the still more powerful superstition of the bridge,—a superstition so interwoven with every thought and hope of the Willamettes that it had become a part of their character as a tribe.

68

And now when their martial enthusiasm and fatalistic courage were all aglow, when the recital of their fathers' deeds had stirred their blood and the portrayal of their own victories filled them again with the fierce joy of conflict, when the mountain of stone that arched the Columbia had risen before them in assurance of dominion as eternal as itself,—now, when in every eye gleamed desire of battle and every heart was aflame, the chief made (and it was characteristic of him) in one terse sentence his crowning appeal,—

"Chiefs, speak your heart. Shall the runners be sent out to call the council?"

There was a moment of intense silence. Then a low, deep murmur of consent came from the excited listeners: a half-smothered war-cry burst from the lips of Mishlah, and the victory was won.

One only sat silent and apart, his robe drawn close, his head bent down, seemingly oblivious of all around him, as if resigned to inevitable doom.

"To-morrow at dawn, while the light is yet young, the runners will go out. Let the chiefs meet here in the grove to hear the message given them to be carried to the tribes. The talk is ended."

CHAPTER II.

THE WAR-CHIEF AND THE SEER.

Cassandra's wild voice prophesying woe.

PHILIP BOURKE MARSTON.

The war-chief left the grove as soon as he had dismissed the council. Tohomish went with him. For some distance they walked together, the one erect and majestic, the other gliding like a shadow by his side.

At length Multnomah stopped under a giant cottonwood and looked sternly at Tohomish.

"You frightened the council to-day with bad *mimaluse* [death] talk. Why did you do it? Why did you bring into a council of warriors dreams fit only for old men that lie sleeping in the sun by the door of the wigwam?"

"I said what my eyes saw and my ears heard, and it was true."

"It cannot be true, for the Great Spirit has said that the Willamettes shall rule the tribes as long as the bridge shall stand; and how can it fall when it is a mountain of stone?"

A strange expression crossed Tohomish's sullen face.

"Multnomah, beware how you rest on the prophecy of the bridge. Lean not your hand on it, for it is 70 as if you put it forth to lean it on a coiled rattlesnake."

"Your sayings are dark," replied the chief impatiently. "Speak plainly."

Tohomish shook his head, and the gloomy look habitual to him came back.

"I cannot. Dreams and omens I can tell, but the secret of the bridge is the secret of the Great Spirit; and I cannot tell it lest he become angry and take from me my power of moving men with burning words."

"The secret of the Great Spirit! What black thing is it you are hiding and covering up with words? Bring it forth into the light, that I may see it."

"No, it is my *tomanowos*. Were I to tell it the gift of eloquence would go from me, the fire would die from my heart and the words from my lips, and my life would wither up within me."

Multnomah was silent. Massive and commanding as was his character he was still an Indian, and the words of the seer had touched the latent superstition in his nature. They referred to that strongest and most powerful of all the strange beliefs of the Oregon savages,—the spirit possession or devil worship of the *tomanowos*.

As soon as an Oregon Indian was old enough to aspire to a place among the braves, he was sent into the hills alone. There he fasted, prayed, and danced, chanted the medicine-chant, and cut himself with knife or thorn till he fell exhausted to the ground. Whatever he saw then, in waking delirium or feverish sleep, was the charm that was to control his future. Be it bird or beast, dream or mystic revelation, 71 it was his *totem* or *tomanowos*, and gave him strength, cunning, or swiftness, sometimes knowledge of the future, imparting to him its own characteristics. But *what* it was, its name or nature, was the one secret that must go with him to his grave. Woe unto him if he told the name of his *totem*. In that moment it would desert him, taking from him all strength and power, leaving him a shattered wreck, an outcast from camp and war-party.

"Multnomah says well that it is a black secret, but it is my *totem* and may not be told. For many winters Tohomish has carried it in his breast, till its poisoned sap has filled his heart with bitterness, till for him gladness and warmth have gone out of the light, laughter has grown a sob of pain, and sorrow and death have become what the feast, the battle, and the chase are to other men. It is the black secret, the secret of the coming trouble, that makes Tohomish's voice like the voice of a pine; so that men say it has in it sweetness and mystery and haunting woe, moving the heart as no other can. And if he tells the secret, eloquence and life go with it. Shall Tohomish tell it? Will Multnomah listen while Tohomish shows what is to befall the bridge and the Willamettes in the time that is to come?"

The war-chief gazed at him earnestly. In that troubled, determined look, superstition struggled for a moment and then gave way to the invincible obstinacy of his resolve.

"No. Multnomah knows that his own heart is strong and will not fail him, come what may; and that is all he cares to know. If you told me, the *tomanowos* would be angry, and drain your spirit 72 from you and cast you aside as the serpent casts its skin. And you must be the most eloquent of all at the great council; for there the arm of Multnomah and the voice of Tohomish must bend the bad chiefs before them."

His accents had the same undertone of arbitrary will, of inflexible determination, that had been in them when he spoke in the council. Though the shadows fell more and more ominous and threatening across his path, to turn back did not occur to him. The stubborn tenacity of the man could not let go his settled purpose.

"Tohomish will be at the council and speak for his chief and his tribe?" asked Multnomah, in a tone that was half inquiry, half command; for the seer whose mysterious power as an orator gave him so strong an influence over the Indians must be there.

Tohomish's haggard and repulsive face had settled back into the look of mournful apathy habitual to him. He had not, since the council, attempted to change the chief's decision by a single word, but seemed to have resigned himself with true Indian fatalism to that which was to come.

"Tohomish will go to the council," he said in those soft and lingering accents, indescribably sweet and sad, with which his degraded face contrasted so strongly. "Yes, he will go to the council, and his voice shall bend and turn the hearts of men as never before. Strong will be the words that he shall say, for with him it will be sunset and his voice will be heard no more."

73

"Where will you go when the council is ended, that we shall see you no more?" asked Multnomah.

"On the death-trail to the spirit-land,—nor will I go alone," was the startling reply; and the seer glided noiselessly away and disappeared among the trees.

74

CHAPTER III.

WALLULAH.

Ne'er   was   seen
In art or nature, aught so passing sweet
As was the form that in its beauteous frame
Inclosed her, and is scattered now in dust.

CAREY: *Dante*.

Multnomah passed on to seek the lodge of his daughter Wallulah, a half Asiatic, and the most beautiful woman in all the land of the Wauna.

Reader, would you know the tale of the fair oriental of whom was born the sweet beauty of Wallulah?

Eighteen years before the time of our story, an East Indian ship was wrecked on the Columbia bar, the crew and cargo falling into the hands of the Indians. Among the rescued was a young and exceedingly lovely woman, who was hospitably entertained by the chief of the tribe. He and his people were deeply impressed by the grace of the fair stranger, whose dainty beauty won for her the name of "Sea-Flower," because the sea, that is ever drifting weeds, had for once wafted a flower to the shore.

As she sat on the mat in the rude bark lodge, the stern chief softened his voice, trying to talk with her; the uncouth women gently stroked her long soft hair, and some of the bolder and more curious touched her white hands wonderingly, while the throng of dusky faces pressed close round the pale, 75 sweet creature whose eyes looked at them with a deep, dumb woe they could not understand.

When she had become familiar with the Willamette tongue, she told them that she was the daughter of a chief far away across the great water, who ruled a country as broad as the land of the Wauna and far richer. He had sent her as a bride to the ruler of another land, with a fabulous dowry of jewels and a thousand gifts besides. But the ship that bore her and her splendid treasures had been turned from its course by a terrible storm. Day after day it was driven through a waste of blackness and foam,—the sails rent, the masts swept away, the shattered hulk hurled onward like a straw by the fury of the wind. When the tempest had spent itself, they found themselves in a strange sea under strange stars. Compass and chart were gone; they knew not where they were, and caught in some unknown current, they could only drift blindly on and on. Never sighting land, seeing naught but the everlasting sweep of wave and sky, it began to be whispered in terror that this ocean had no further shore, that they might sail on forever, seeing nothing but the boundless waters. At length, when the superstitious sailors began to talk of throwing their fair charge overboard as an offering to the gods, the blue peaks of the Coast Range rose out of the water, and the ever rain-freshened green of the Oregon forests dawned upon them. Then came the attempt to enter the Columbia, and the wreck on the bar.[1]

76

Multnomah made the lovely princess his wife, and Sea-Flower showed the spirit of a queen. She tried to introduce among the Indians something of the refinement of her oriental home. From her the degraded medicine-men and dreamers caught a gleam of the majestic lore of Buddha; to the chiefs-in-council she taught something of the grave, inexorable justice of the East, that seemed like a higher development of their own grim unwritten code. Her influence was very great, for she was naturally eloquent and of noble presence. More than one sachem felt the inspiration of better, purer thoughts than he had ever known before when the "war-chief's woman" spoke in council. Strange gatherings were those: blood-stained chiefs and savage warriors listening all intent to the sweetest of Indian tongues spoken in modulations that were music; the wild heart of the empire stirred by the perfumed breath of a woman!

She had died three years before the events we have been narrating, and had left to her daughter the heritage of her refinement and her beauty. 77 Wallulah was the only child of the war-chief and his Asiatic wife, the sole heir of her father's sovereignty.

Two miles from the council grove, in the interior of the island, was Wallulah's lodge. The path that Multnomah took led through a pleasant sylvan lawn. The grass was green, and the air full of the scent of buds and flowers. Here and there a butterfly floated like a sunbeam through the woodland shadows, and a humming-bird darted in winged beauty from bloom to bloom. The lark's song came vibrating through the air, and in the more open spaces innumerable birds flew twittering in the sun. The dewy freshness, the exquisite softness of spring, was everywhere.

In the golden weather, through shadowed wood and sunny opening, the war-chief sought his daughter's lodge.

Suddenly a familiar sound attracted his attention, and he turned toward it. A few steps, and he came to the margin of a small lake. Several snow-white swans were floating on it; and near the edge of the water, but concealed from the swans by the tall reeds that grew along the shore, was his daughter, watching them.

She was attired in a simple dress of some oriental fabric. Her form was small and delicately moulded; her long black hair fell in rich masses about her shoulders; and her profile, turned toward him, was sweetly feminine. The Indian type showed plainly, but was softened with her mother's grace. Her face was sad, with large appealing eyes and mournful lips, and full of haunting loveliness; a face whose strange mournfulness was deepened by the splendor of its 78 beauty; a face the like of which is rarely seen, but once seen can never be forgotten.

There was something despondent even in her pose, as she sat with her shoulders drooping slightly forward and her dark eyes fixed absently on the swans, watching them through the bending reeds. Now one uttered its note, and she listened, seeming to vibrate to the deep, plaintive cry; then she raised to her lips a flute that she held in her hands, and answered it with a perfect intonation,—an intonation that breathed the very spirit of the swan. So successful was the mimicry that the swans replied, thinking it the cry of a hidden mate; and again she softly, rhythmically responded.

"Wallulah!" said the chief.

She sprang to her feet and turned toward him. Her dark face lighted with an expressive flash, her black eyes shone, her features glowed with joy and surprise. It was like the breaking forth of an inner illumination. There was now nothing of the Indian in her face.

"My father!" she exclaimed, springing to him and kissing his hand, greeting him as her mother had taught her to do from childhood. "Welcome! Were you searching for me?"

"Yes, you were well hidden, but Multnomah is a good hunter and can always track the fawn to its covert," replied the chief, with the faint semblance of a smile. All that there was of gentleness in his nature came out when talking with his daughter.

"You have come from the council? Are you not weary and hungry? Come to the lodge, and let Wallulah 79 give you food, and spread a mat for you to rest upon."

"No, I am hungry only to see Wallulah and hear her talk. Sit down on the log again." She seated herself, and her father stood beside her with an abstracted gaze, his hand stroking her long, soft tresses. He was thinking of the darker, richer tresses of another, whose proud, sad face and mournful eyes with their wistful meaning, so like Wallulah's own, he, a barbarian prince, could never understand.

Although, according to the superstitious custom of the Willamettes, he never spoke the name of Sea-Flower or alluded to her in any way, he loved his lost wife with a deep and unchanging affection. She had been a fair frail thing whose grace and refinement perplexed and fascinated him, moving him to unwonted tenderness and yearning. He had brought to her the spoils of the chase and of battle. The finest mat was braided for her lodge, the choicest skins and furs spread for her bed, and the chieftainess's string of *hiagua* shells and grizzly bear's claws had been put around her white neck by Multnomah's own hand. In spite of all this, she drooped and saddened year by year; the very hands that sought to cherish her seemed but to bruise; and she sickened and died, the delicate woman, in the arms of the iron war-chief, like a flower in the grasp of a mailed hand.

Why did she die? Why did she always seem so sad? Why did she so often steal away to weep over her child? Was not the best food hers, and the warm place by the lodge fire, and the softest bearskin to rest on; and was she not the wife of Multnomah,—the 80 big chief's woman? Why then should she droop and die like a winged bird that one tries to tame by tying it to the wigwam stake and tossing it food?

Often the old chief brooded over these questions, but it was unknown to all, even to Wallulah. Only his raven tresses, cut close year by year in sign of perpetual mourning, told that he had not forgotten, could never forget.

The swans had taken flight, and their long lingering note sounded faint in the distance.

"You have frightened away my swans," said Wallulah, looking up at him smilingly.

A shadow crossed his brow.

"Wallulah," he said, and his voice had now the stern ring habitual to it, "you waste your life with the birds and trees and that thing of sweet sounds,"—pointing to the flute. "Better be learning to think on the things a war-chief's daughter should care for,—the feast and the council, the war-parties and the welcome to the braves when they come back to the camp with the spoil."

The bright look died out of her face.

"You say those words so often," she replied sorrowfully, "and I try to obey, but cannot. War is terrible to me."

His countenance grew harsher, his hand ceased to stroke her hair.

"And has Multnomah, chief of the Willamettes and war-chief of the Wauna, lived to hear his daughter say that war is terrible to her?

Have you nothing of your father in you? Remember the tales of the brave women of Multnomah's race,—the women 81 whose blood is in your veins. Remember that they spoke burning words in the council, and went forth with the men to battle, and came back with their own garments stained with blood. You shudder! Is it at the thought of blood?"

The old wistful look came back, the old sadness was on the beautiful face again. One could see now why it was there.

"My father," she said sorrowfully, "Wallulah has tried to love those things, but she cannot. She cannot change the heart the Great Spirit has given her. She cannot bring herself to be a woman of battle any more than she can sound a war-cry on her flute," and she lifted it as she spoke.

He took it into his own hands.

"It is this," he said, breaking down the sensitive girl in the same despotic way in which he bent the wills of warriors; "it is this that makes you weak. Is it a charm that draws the life from your heart? If so, it can be broken."

Another moment and the flute would have been broken in his ruthless hands and its fragments flung into the lake; but Wallulah, startled, caught it from him with a plaintive cry.

"It was my mother's. If you break it you will break my heart!"

The chief's angry features quivered at the mention of her mother, and he instantly released the flute. Wallulah clasped it to her bosom as if it represented in some way the mother she had lost, and her eyes filled with tears. Again her father's hand rested on her head, and she knew that he too was thinking of her mother. Her nature rose up in revolt against the 82 Indian custom which forbade talking of the dead. Oh, if she might only talk with her father about her mother, though it were but a few brief words! Never since her mother's death had her name been mentioned between them. She lifted her eyes, pathetic with three years' hunger, to his. As their glances met, it seemed as if the veil that had been between their diverse natures was for a moment lifted, and they understood each other better than they ever had before. While his look imposed silence and sealed her lips as with a spoken command, there was a gleam of tenderness in it that said, "I understand, I too remember; but it must not be spoken."

There came to her a sense of getting closer to her father's heart, even while his eyes held her back and bade her be silent.

At length the chief spoke, this time very gently.

"Now I shall talk to you not as to a girl but as to a woman. You are Multnomah's only child. When he dies there will be no one but you to take his place. Are your shoulders strong enough to bear the weight of power, the weight that crushes men? Can you break down revolt and read the hearts of plotters,—yes, and detect conspiracy when it is but a whisper in the air? Can you sway council and battle to your will as the warrior bends his bow? No; it takes men, men strong of heart, to rule the races of the Wauna. Therefore there is but one way left me whereby the line of Multnomah may still be head of the confederacy when he is gone. I must wed you to a great warrior who can take my place when I am dead and shelter you with his strength. Then the name and the power of Multnomah will still live 83 among the tribes, though Multnomah himself be crumbled into dust."

She made no reply, but sat looking confused and pained, by no means elated at the future he had described.

"Have you never thought of this,—that some time I must give you to a warrior?"

Her head drooped lower and her cheek faintly flushed.

"Sometimes."

"But you have chosen no one?"

"I do not know," she faltered.

Her father's hand still rested on her head, but there was an expression on his face that showed he would not hesitate to sacrifice her happiness to his ambition.

"You have chosen, then? Is he a chief? No, I will not ask that; the daughter of Multnomah could love no one but a chief. I have already selected a husband for you. Tear this other love from your heart and cast it aside."

The flush died out of her cheek, leaving it cold and ashen; and her fingers worked nervously with the flute in her lap.

He continued coldly,—

"The fame of your beauty has gone out through all the land. The chief of the Chopponish[2] has offered many horses for you, and the chief of the Spokanes, our ancient foes, has said there would be peace between us if I gave you to him. But I have promised you to another. Your marriage to him will knit the bravest tribe of the confederacy to us; he will take 84 my place when I am dead, and our people will still be strong."

She made no reply. What could she do against her father's granite will? All the grace and mobility were gone from her face, and it was drooping and dull almost to impassiveness. She was only an Indian girl now, waiting to learn the name of him who was to be her master.

"What is the name of the one you love? Speak it once, then never speak it again."

"Snoqualmie, chief of the Cayuses," faltered her tremulous lips.

A quick change of expression came into the gaze that was bent on her.

"Now lift your head and meet your fate like the daughter of a chief. Do not let me see your face change while I tell you whom I have chosen."

She lifted her face in a tumult of fear and dread, and her eyes fastened pathetically on the chief.

"His name is—" she clasped her hands and her whole soul went out to her father in the mute supplication of her gaze—"the chief Snoqualmie, him of whom you have thought."

Her face was bewilderment itself for an instant; the next, the sudden light, the quick flash of expression which transfigured it in a moment of joy or surprise, came to her, and she raised his hand and kissed it. Was that all? Remember she had in her the deep, mute Indian nature that meets joy or anguish alike in silence. She had early learned to repress and control her emotions. Perhaps that was why she was so sad and brooding now.

85

"Where have you seen Snoqualmie?" asked Multnomah. "Not in your father's lodge, surely, for when strange chiefs came to him you always fled like a frightened bird."

"Once only have I seen him," she replied, flushing and confused. "He had come here alone to tell you that some of the tribes were plotting against you. I saw him as he went back through the wood to the place where his canoe was drawn up on the bank of the river. He was tall; his black hair fell below his shoulders; and his look was very proud and strong. His back was to the setting sun, and it shone around him robing him with fire, and I thought he looked like the Indian sun-god."

"I am glad it is pleasant for you to obey me. Now, listen while I tell you what you must do as the wife of Snoqualmie."

Stilling the sweet tumult in her breast, she tried hard to listen while he told her of the plans, the treaties, the friendships, and the enmities she must urge on her husband, when he became war-chief and was carrying on her father's work; and in part she understood, for her imagination was captivated by the splendid though barbarian dream of empire he set before her.

At length, as the sun was setting, one came to tell Multnomah that a runner from a tribe beyond the mountains had come to see him. Then her father left her; but Wallulah still sat on the mossy log, while all the woodland was golden in the glory of sunset.

Her beloved flute was pressed close to her cheek, and her face was bright and joyous; she was thinking of Snoqualmie, the handsome stately chief whom 86 she had seen but once, but whose appearance, as she saw him then, had filled her girlish heart.

And all the time she knew not that this Snoqualmie, to whom she was to be given, was one of the most cruel and inhuman of men, terrible even to the grim warriors of the Wauna for his deeds of blood.

---

[1]

Shipwrecks of Asiatic vessels are not uncommon on the Pacific Coast, several having occurred during the present century,—notably that of a Japanese junk in 1833, from which three passengers were saved at the hands of the Indians; while the cases of beeswax that have been disinterred on the sea-coast, the oriental words that are found ingrafted in the native languages, and the Asiatic type of countenance shown by many of the natives, prove such wrecks to have been frequent in prehistoric times. One of the most romantic stories of the Oregon coast is that which the Indians tell of a buried treasure at Mount Nehalem, left there generations ago by shipwrecked men of strange garb and curious arms,—treasure which, like that of Captain Kidd, has been often sought but never found. There is also an Indian legend of a shipwrecked white man named Soto, and his comrades (See Mrs. Victor's "Oregon and Washington"), who lived long with the mid-Columbia Indians and then left them to seek some settlement of their own people in the south. All of these legends point to the not infrequent occurrence of such a wreck as our story describes.

[2]

Indian name of the Nez Percés.

CHAPTER IV.

SENDING OUT THE RUNNERS.

Speed, Malise, speed; the dun deer's hide
On fleeter foot was never tied;
Herald of battle, fate and fear
Stretch around thy fleet career.

SCOTT.

At early morning, the sachems had gathered in the council-grove, Multnomah on the seat of the war-chief, and twenty runners before him. They were the flower of the Willamette youth, every one of royal birth, handsome in shape and limb, fleet-footed as the deer. They were slender and sinewy in build, with aquiline features and sharp searching eyes.

Their garb was light. Leggins and moccasins had been laid aside; even the *hiagua* shells were stripped from their ears. All stood nerved and eager for the race, waiting for the word that was to scatter them throughout the Indian empire, living thunderbolts bearing the summons of Multnomah.

The message had been given them, and they waited only to pledge themselves to its faithful delivery.

"You promise," said the chief, while his flashing glance read every messenger to the heart, "you promise that neither cougar nor cataract nor ambuscade shall deter you from the delivery of this summons; that you will not turn back, though the spears 88 of the enemy are thicker in your path than ferns along the Santiam? You promise that though you fall in death, the summons shall go on?"

The spokesman of the runners, the runner to the Chopponish, stepped forward. With gestures of perfect grace, and in a voice that rang like a silver trumpet, he repeated the ancient oath of the Willamettes,—the oath used by the Shoshones to-day.

"The earth hears us, the sun sees us. Shall we fail in fidelity to our chief?"

There was a pause. The distant cry of swans came from the river; the great trees of council rustled in the breeze. Multnomah rose from his seat, gripping the bow on which he leaned. Into that one moment he seemed gathering yet repressing all the fierceness of his passion, all the grandeur of his will. Far in the shade he saw Tohomish raise his hand imploringly, but the eyes of the orator sank once more under the glance of the war-chief.

"Go!"

An electric shock passed through all who heard; and except for the chiefs standing on its outskirts like sombre shadows, the grove was empty in a moment.

Beyond the waters that girdled the island, one runner took the trail to Puyallup, one the trail to Umatilla, one the path to Chelon, and one the path to Shasta; another departed toward the volcano-rent desert of Klamath, and still another toward the sea-washed shores of Puget Sound.

The irrevocable summons had gone forth; the council was inevitable,—the crisis must come.

"The Earth hears us, the Sun sees us."

89

Long did Multnomah and his chiefs sit in council that day. Resolute were the speeches that came from all, though many secretly regretted that they had allowed Multnomah's oratory to persuade them into declaring for the council: but there was no retreat.

Across hills and canyons sped the fleet runners, on to the huge bark lodges of Puget Sound, the fisheries of the Columbia, and the crowded race-courses of the Yakima. Into camps of wandering prairie tribes, where the lodges stood like a city to-day and were rolled up and strapped on the backs of horses to-morrow; into councils where sinister chiefs were talking low of war against the Willamettes; into wild midnight dances of plotting dreamers and medicine-men,—they came with the brief stern summons, and passed on to speak it to the tribes beyond.

BOOK III.

THE GATHERING OF THE TRIBES.

CHAPTER I.

THE BROKEN PEACE-PIPE.

My full defiance, hate, and scorn.

SCOTT.

It is the day after the departure of the runners to call the great council,—eight years since Cecil Grey went out into the wilderness. Smoke is curling slowly upward from an Indian camp on the prairie not far from the Blue Mountains of eastern Oregon. Fifteen or twenty cone-shaped lodges, each made of mats stretched on a framework of poles, compose the village. It swarms with wolfish-looking dogs and dirty, unclad children. Heaps of refuse, heads and feet of game, lie decaying among the wigwams, tainting the air with their disgusting odor. Here and there an ancient withered specimen of humanity sits in the sun, absorbing its rays with a dull animal-like sense of enjoyment, and a group of warriors lie idly talking. Some of the squaws are preparing food, boiling it in water-tight willow baskets by filling them with water and putting in hot stones.[3] Horses are 92 tethered near the lodges, and others are running loose on the prairie.

There are not many of them. The Indians have only scores now where a century later Lewis and Clark found thousands; and there are old men in the camp who can recall the time when the first horses ever seen among them were bought or stolen from the tribes to the south.

On every side the prairie sweeps away in long grassy swells and hollows, rolling off to the base of the Blue Mountains.

The camp has the sluggish aspect that an Indian camp always presents at noonday.

Suddenly a keen-sighted warrior points to a dim speck far over the prairie toward the land of the Bannocks. A white man would have scarcely noticed it; or if he had, would have thought it only some wandering deer or antelope. But the Indians, glancing at the moving object, have already recognized it as a horseman coming straight toward the camp.

Some messenger it is, doubtless, from the Bannocks. Once the whole camp would have rushed to arms at the approach of a rider from that direction, for the two tribes had been at bitter enmity; but of late the peace-pipe has been smoked between them, and the old feud is at an end. Still, the sight arouses considerable curiosity and much speculation as to the object of the visitor.

He is a good rider, his horse is fleet, and in less time than would have been thought possible reaches the camp. He gallops up, stops near the lodges that are farthest out, and springs lightly to the ground. He does not go on into the camp, but stands beside 93 his horse till advances are made on the other side.

The dogs bark at him; his steed, a fiery black, tosses its head and paws the ground; he stands beside it immovably, and to all appearance is ready so to stand till sunset. Some of the warriors recognize him as one of the bravest of the Bannocks. He looks like a daring, resolute man, yet wary and self-contained.

After a while one of the Cayuse warriors (for this was a camp of the Cayuses) advanced toward him, and a grave salutation was exchanged. Then the Bannock said that he wanted to see the Cayuse chief, Snoqualmie, in the council-lodge, for the chief of the Bannocks had sent a "talk" to the Cayuses.

The warrior left him to speak with Snoqualmie. In a short time he returned, saying that the chief and the warriors had gone to the council-lodge and were ready to hear the "talk" that their brother, the chief of the Bannocks, had sent them. The messenger tied his horse by its lariat, or long hair-rope, to a bush, and followed the brave to the lodge.

It was a large wigwam in the centre of the village. A crowd of old men, women, and children had already gathered around the door. Within, on one side of the room, sat in three rows a semi-circle of braves, facing the chief, who sat on the opposite side. Near the door was a clear space where the messenger was to stand while speaking.

He entered, and the doorway behind him was immediately blocked up by the motley crowd excluded from the interior. Not a warrior in the council looked at him; even the chief, Snoqualmie, did not turn his head. The messenger advanced a few paces into the 94 room, stopped, and stood as impassive as the rest. Then, when the demands of Indian stoicism had been satisfied, Snoqualmie turned his face, a handsome but treacherous and cruel face, upon the messenger.

"The warrior comes to speak the words of our brother, the chief of the Bannocks; he is welcome. Shall we smoke the pipe of peace before we hear our brother's words?"

The Bannock gazed steadily at Snoqualmie. In that fierce and proud regard was something the Cayuse could not fathom.

"Why should the peace-pipe be smoked?" he asked. "Was it not smoked in the great council a moon ago? Did not Snoqualmie say then that the two tribes should henceforth be as one tribe, and that the Bannocks should be the brethren of the Cayuses forever?"

"Those were the words," replied the chief with dignity. "Snoqualmie has not forgotten them."

All eyes were now turned on the messenger; they saw that something unexpected was coming. The Bannock drew his form up to its full height, and his resolute features expressed the bitterest scorn.

"Nor have the Bannocks forgotten. At the council you talked 'peace, peace.' Last night some of your young men surprised a little camp of Bannocks,—a few old men and boys who were watching horses,—and slew them and ran off the horses. Is that your peace? The Bannocks will have no such peace. *This* is the word the chief of the Bannocks sends you!"

Holding up the peace-pipe that had been smoked at the great council and afterward given to the medicine-men of the Bannocks as a pledge of Cayuse sincerity, 95 he broke the long slender stem twice, thrice, crushed the bowl in his fingers, and dashed the pieces at Snoqualmie's feet. It was a defiance, a contemptuous rejection of peace, a declaration of war more disdainful than any words could have made it.

Then, before they could recover from their astonishment, the Bannock turned and leaped through the crowd at the door,—for an instant's stay was death. Even as he leaped, Snoqualmie's tomahawk whizzed after him, and a dozen warriors were on their feet, weapon in hand. But the swift, wild drama had been played like lightning, and he was gone. Only, a brave who had tried to intercept his passage lay on the ground outside the lodge, stabbed to the heart. They rushed to the door in time to see him throw himself on his horse and dash off, looking back to give a yell of triumph and defiance.

In less time than it takes to describe it, the horses tethered near the lodges were mounted and twenty riders were in pursuit. But the Bannock was considerably in advance now, and the fine black horse he rode held its own nobly. Out over the prairie flew the pursuing Cayuses, yelling like demons, the fugitive turning now and then to utter a shout of derision.

Back at the lodges, the crowd of spectators looked on with excited comments.

"His horse is tired, ours are fresh!" "They gain on him!" "No, he is getting farther from them!" "See, he throws away his blanket!" "They are closer, closer!" "No, no, his horse goes like a deer."

Out over the prairies, fleeting like the shadow of a hurrying cloud, passed the race, the black horse 96 leading, the Cayuse riders close behind, their long hair outstreaming, their moccasins pressed against their horses' sides, their whips falling without mercy. Down a canyon they swept in pursuit and passed from the ken of the watchers at the camp, the black horse still in the van.

But it could not cope with the fresh horses of the Cayuses, and they gained steadily. At last the pursuers came within bowshot, but they did not shoot; the fugitive knew too well the reason why. Woe unto him if he fell alive into their hands! He leaned low along his horse's neck, chanting a weird refrain as if charming it to its utmost speed, and ever and anon looked back with that heart-shaking shout of defiance. But steadily his pursuers gained on him; and one, outstripping the rest, rode alongside and reached out to seize his rein. Even as he touched it, the Bannock's war-club swung in air and the Cayuse reeled dead from his saddle. A howl of rage burst from the others, a whoop of exultation from the fugitive.

But at length his horse's breath grew short and broken, he felt its body tremble as it ran, and his enemies closed in around him.

Thrice the war-club rose and fell, thrice was a saddle emptied; but all in vain. Quickly his horse was caught, he was dragged from the saddle and bound hand and foot.

He was thrown across a horse and brought back to the village. What a chorus of triumph went up from the camp, when it was seen that they were bringing him back! It was an ominous sound, with something of wolfish ferocity in it. But the Bannock only smiled grimly.

97

He is bound to a post,—a charred, bloodstained post to which others of his race have been bound before him. The women and children taunt him, jeer at him, strike him even. The warriors do not. They will presently do more than that. Some busy themselves building a fire near by; others bring pieces of flint, spear points, jagged fragments of rock, and heat them in it. The prisoner, dusty, torn, parched with thirst, and bleeding from many wounds, looks on with perfect indifference. Snoqualmie comes and gazes at him; the prisoner does not notice him, is seemingly unconscious of his presence.

By and by a band of hunters ride up from a long excursion. They have heard nothing of the trouble. With them is a young Bannock who is visiting the tribe. He rides up with his Cayuse comrades, laughing, gesticulating in a lively way. The jest dies on his lips when he recognizes the Bannock who is tied to the stake. Before he can even think of flight, he is dragged from his horse and bound,—his whilom comrades, as soon as they understand the situation, becoming his bitterest assailants.

For it is war again, war to the death between the tribes, until, two centuries later, both shall alike be crushed by the white man.

At length the preparations are complete, and the women and children, who have been swarming around and taunting the captives, are brushed aside like so many flies by the stern warriors. First, the young Bannock who has just come in is put where he must have a full view of the other. Neither speaks, but a glance passes between them that is like a mutual charge to die bravely. Snoqualmie comes and stands 98 close by the prisoner and gives directions for the torture to begin.

The Bannock is stripped. The stone blades that have been in the fire are brought, all red and glowing with heat, and pressed against his bare flesh. It burns and hisses under the fiery torture, but the warrior only sneers.

"It doesn't hurt; you can't hurt me. You are fools. You don't know how to torture."[4]

No refinement of cruelty could wring a complaint from him. It was in vain that they burned him, cut the flesh from his fingers, branded his cheek with the heated bowl of the pipe he had broken.

"Try it again," he said mockingly, while his flesh smoked. "I feel no pain. We torture your people a great deal better, for we make them cry out like little children."

More and more murderous and terrible grew the wrath of his tormentors, as this stream of vituperation fell on their ears. Again and again weapons were lifted to slay him, but Snoqualmie put them back.

"He can suffer more yet," he said; and the words were like a glimpse into the cold, merciless heart of the man. Other and fiercer tortures were devised by the chief, who stood over him, pointing out where and how the keenest pain could be given, the bitterest pang inflicted on that burned and broken body. At last it seemed no longer a man, but a bleeding, scorched, mutilated mass of flesh that hung to the stake; only the lips still breathed defiance and the eyes gleamed deathless hate. Looking upon one and 99 another, he boasted of how he had slain their friends and relatives. Many of his boasts were undoubtedly false, but they were very bitter.

"It was by my arrow that you lost your eye," he said to one; "I scalped your father," to another; and every taunt provoked counter-taunts accompanied with blows.

At length he looked at Snoqualmie,—a look so ghastly, so disfigured, that it was like something seen in a horrible dream.

"I took your sister prisoner last winter; you never knew,—you thought she had wandered from home and was lost in a storm. We put out her eyes, we tore out her tongue, and then we told her to go out in the snow and find food. Ah-h-h! you should have seen her tears as she went out into the storm, and—"

The sentence was never finished. While the last word lingered on his lips, his body sunk into a lifeless heap under a terrific blow, and Snoqualmie put back his blood-stained tomahawk into his belt.

"Shall we kill the other?" demanded the warriors, gathering around the surviving Bannock, who had been a stoical spectator of his companion's sufferings. A ferocious clamor from the women and children hailed the suggestion of new torture; they thronged around the captive, the children struck him, the women abused him, spat upon him even, but not a muscle of his face quivered; he merely looked at them with stolid indifference.

"Kill him, kill him!" "Stretch him on red hot stones!" "We will make *him* cry!"

Snoqualmie hesitated. He wished to save this man for another purpose, and yet the Indian blood-thirst 100 was on him; chief and warrior alike were drunken with fury, mad with the lust of cruelty.

As he hesitated, a white man clad in the garb of an Indian hunter pushed his way through the crowd. Silence fell upon the throng; the clamor of the women, the fierce questioning of the warriors ceased. The personality of this man was so full of tenderness and sympathy, so strong and commanding, that it impressed the most savage nature. Amid the silence, he came and looked first at the dead body that yet hung motionless from the stake, then sorrowfully, reproachfully, at the circle of faces around. An expression half of sullen shame, half of defiance, crossed more than one countenance as his glance fell upon it.

"Friends," said he, sadly, pointing at the dead, "is this your peace with the Bannocks,—the peace you prayed the Great Spirit to bless, the peace that was to last forever?"

"The Bannocks sent back the peace-pipe by this man, and he broke it and cast the pieces in our teeth," answered one, stubbornly.

"And you slew him for it? Why not have sent runners to his tribe asking why it was returned, and demanding to know what wrong you had done, that you might right it? Now there will be war. When you lie down to sleep at night, the surprise may be on you and massacre come while your eyes are heavy with slumber; when you are gone on the buffalo trail the tomahawk may fall on the women and children at home. Death will lurk for you in every thicket and creep round every encampment. The Great Spirit is angry because you have stained your hands in blood without cause."

101

There was no reply. This white man, coming from far eastern lands lying they knew not where, who told them God had sent him to warn them to be better, had a singular influence over them. There was none of his hearers who did not dimly feel that he had done wrong in burning and scarring the poor mass of humanity before him, and that the Great Spirit was angry with him for it.

Back in the crowd, some of the children, young demons hungering for blood, began to clamor again for the death of the surviving Bannock. Cecil Grey looked at him pityingly.

"At least you can let him go."

There was no answer. Better impulses, better desires, were struggling in their degraded minds; but cruelty was deeply rooted within them, the vague shame and misgiving his words had roused was not so strong as the dark animalism of their natures.

Cecil turned to Snoqualmie.

"I saved your life once, will you not give me his?"

The chief regarded him coldly.

"Take it," he said after a pause. Cecil stooped over and untied the thongs that bound the captive, who rose to his feet amid a low angry murmur from those around. Snoqualmie silenced it with an imperious gesture. Then he turned to the young Bannock.

"Dog, one of a race of dogs! go back to your people and tell them what you have seen to-day. Tell them how we burned and tortured their messenger, and that we let you go only to tell the tale. Tell them, too, that Snoqualmie knows his sister died by their hand last winter, and that for every hair upon 102 her head he will burn a Bannock warrior at the stake. Go, and be quick, lest my war-party overtake you on the trail."

The Bannock left without a word, taking the trail across the prairie toward the land of his tribe.

"The gift was given, but there was that given with it that made it bitter. And now may I bury this dead body?"

"It is only a Bannock; who cares what is done with it?" replied Snoqualmie. "But remember, my debt is paid. Ask of me no more gifts," and the chief turned abruptly away.

"Who will help me bury this man?" asked Cecil. No one replied; and he went alone and cut the thongs that bound the body to the stake. But as he stooped to raise it, a tall fine-looking man, a renegade from the Shoshones, who had taken no part in the torture, came forward to help him. Together they bore the corpse away from the camp to the hillside; together they hollowed out a shallow grave and stretched the body in it, covering it with earth and heaping stones on top, that the cayote might not disturb the last sleep of the dead.

When they returned to the camp, they found a war-party already in the saddle, with Snoqualmie at their head, ready to take the Bannock trail. But before they left the camp, a runner entered it with a summons from Multnomah calling them to the great council of the tribes on Wappatto Island, for which they must start on the morrow.

---

[3]

See Bancroft's "Native Races," vol. i., p. 270.

[4]

See Ross Cox's "Adventures on the Columbia River" for a description of torture among the Columbia tribes.

CHAPTER II.

ON THE WAY TO THE COUNCIL.

They arrived at the village of Wishram.

IRVING: *Astoria.*

The camp was all astir at dawn, for sunset must see them far on the way. They must first cross the prairies to the northward till they struck the Columbia, then take the great trail leading down it to the Willamette valley. It was a two days' journey at the least.

Squaws were preparing a hurried meal; lodge-poles were being taken down and the mats that covered them rolled up and strapped on the backs of horses; Indians, yelling and vociferating, were driving up bands of horses from which pack and riding ponies were to be selected; unbroken animals were rearing and plunging beneath their first burdens, while mongrel curs ran barking at their heels. Here and there unskilful hands were throwing the lasso amid the jeers and laughter of the spectators. All was tumult and excitement.

At length they were under way. First rode the squaws, driving before them pack-horses and ponies, for the herds and entire movable property of the tribe accompanied it in all its marches. The squaws rode astride, like men, in the rude wooden saddles that one yet sees used by the wilder Indians of eastern 104 Oregon and Idaho,—very high, both before and behind, looking like exaggerated pack-saddles. A hair rope, tied around the lower jaw of the horse, answered for a bridle. To this must be added the quirt, a short double-lashed whip fastened into a hollow and curiously carved handle. The application of this whip was so constant as to keep the right arm in continual motion; so that even to-day on the frontier an Indian rider can be distinguished from a white man, at a distance, by the constant rising and falling of the whip arm. With the squaws were the children, some of whom, not over four, five, and six years of age, rode alone on horseback, tied in the high saddles; managing their steeds with instinctive skill, and when the journey became fatiguing, going to sleep, secured by their fastenings from falling off.

Next came the men, on the best horses, unencumbered by weight of any kind and armed with bow and arrow. Here and there a lance pointed with flint, a stone knife or hatchet, or a heavy war-club, hung at the saddle; but the bow and arrow constituted their chief weapon.

The men formed a kind of rear-guard, protecting the migrating tribe from any sudden assault on the part of the Bannocks. There were perhaps two hundred fighting-men in all. Snoqualmie was at their head, and beside him rode the young Willamette runner who had brought the summons from Multnomah the day before. The Willamette was on horseback for the first time in his life. The inland or prairie tribes of eastern Oregon, coming as they did in contact with tribes whose neighbors bordered on Mexico, had owned horses for perhaps a generation; but the sea-board 105 tribes owned very few, and there were tribes on Puget Sound and at the mouth of the Columbia who had never seen them. Even the Willamettes, sovereign tribe of the confederacy though they were, had but few horses.

This morning the young Willamette had bought a colt, giving for it a whole string of *hiagua* shells. It was a pretty, delicate thing, and he was proud of it, and had shown his pride by slitting its ears and cutting off its tail, as was the barbarous custom with many of the Indians. He sat on the little creature now; and loaded as it was with the double weight of himself and the heavy wooden saddle, it could hardly keep pace with the older and stronger horses.

In the rear of all rode Cecil Grey and the Shoshone renegade who had helped him bury the dead Bannock the evening before. Cecil's form was as slight and graceful in its Indian garb as in days gone by, and his face was still the handsome, sensitive face it had been eight years before. It was stronger now, more resolute and mature, and from long intercourse with the Indians there had come into it something grave and Indian-like; but it only gave more of dignity to his mien. His brown beard swept his breast, and his face was bronzed; but the lips quivered under the beard, and the cheek flushed and paled under the bronze.

What had he been doing in the eight years that had elapsed since he left his New England home? Let us listen to his story in his own words as he tells it to the Shoshone renegade by his side.

"I lived in a land far to the east, beside a great water. My people were white like myself. I was one of an order of men whom the Great Spirit had 106 appointed to preach of goodness, mercy, and truth, and to explain to the people the sayings of a mighty book which he had given to the fathers,—a book that told how men should live in this world, and said that a beautiful place in the next would be given those who are good and true in this. But by and by the Great Spirit began to whisper to me of the Indians in the wilderness who knew nothing of the book or the hope within it, and a longing rose within me to go and tell them; but there were ties that held me to my own people, and I knew not what to do. Death cut those ties; and in my hour of grief there came to me a vision of a great bridge far in the west, and of Indians passing over it, and a voice spoke to me and bade me go and seek the land of the bridge, for the Great Spirit had a mission for me there; and I went forth into the wilderness. I met many tribes and tarried with them, telling them of God. Many were evil and treated me harshly, others were kind and listened. Some loved me and wished me to abide always in their lodges and be one of them. But even while they spoke the Great Spirit whispered to me to go on, and an unrest rose within me, and I could not stay.

"So the years went by, and I wandered farther and farther to the west, across rivers and deserts, till I reached this tribe; and they said that farther on, toward the land of the Willamettes, a great river flowed through the mountains, and across it was a bridge of stone built by the gods when the world was young. Then I knew that it was the bridge of my vision, and the unrest came back and I arose to go. But the tribe kept me, half as guest and half as prisoner, 107 and would not let me depart; until last night the runner came summoning them to the council. Now they go, taking me with them. I shall see the land of the bridge and perform the work the Great Spirit has given me to do."

The old grand enthusiasm shone in his look as he closed. The Shoshone regarded him with grave attention.

"What became of the book that told of God?" he asked earnestly.

"A chief took it from me and burned it; but its words were written on my heart, and they could not be destroyed."

They rode on for a time in silence. The way was rugged, the country a succession of canyons and ridges covered with green and waving grass but bare of trees. Behind them, the Blue Mountains were receding in the distance. To the west, Mt. Hood, the great white "Witch Mountain" of the Indians, towered over the prairie, streaking the sky with a long floating wreath of volcanic smoke. Before them, as they journeyed northward toward the Columbia, stretched out the endless prairie. Now they descended into a deep ravine, now they toiled up a steep hillside. The country literally rolled, undulating in immense ridges around and over which the long file of squaws and warriors, herds and pack-horses, wound like a serpent. From the bands ahead came shouts and outcries,—the sounds of rude merriment; and above all the long-drawn intonation so familiar to those who have been much with Indian horsemen,—the endlessly repeated "ho-ha, ho-ha, ho-ha," a kind of crude riding-song.

108

After a while Cecil said, "I have told you the story of my life, will you not tell me the story of yours?"

"Yes," said the renegade, after a moment's thought; "you have shown me your heart as if you were my brother. Now I will show you mine.

"I was a Shoshone warrior.[5] There was a girl in our village whom I had loved from childhood. We played together; we talked of how, when I became a man and a warrior, she should become my wife;

she should keep my wigwam; we would always love one another. She grew up, and the chief offered many horses for her. Her father took them. She became the chief's wife, and all my heart withered up. Everything grew dark. I sat in my wigwam or wandered in the forest, caring for nothing.

"When I met her, she turned her face aside, for was she not the wife of another? Yet I knew her heart hungered for me. The chief knew it too, and when he spoke to her a cloud was ever on his brow and sharp lightning on his tongue. But she was true. Whose lodge was as clean as his? The wood was always carried, the water at hand, the meat cooked. She searched the very thought that was in his heart to save him the trouble of speaking. He could never say, 'Why is it not done?' But her heart was mine, and he knew it; and he treated her like a dog and not like a wife.

"Me too he tried to tread under foot. One day we assembled to hunt the buffalo. Our horses were all collected. Mine stood before my tent, and he came and took them away, saying that they were his. What could I do? He was a chief.

The Great "Witch Mountain" of the Indians.

109

"I came no more to the council, I shared no more in the hunt and the war-dance. I was unhorsed, degraded, dishonored. He told his wife what he had done, and when she wept he beat her.

"One evening I stood on a knoll overlooking the meadow where the horses were feeding; the chief's horses were there, and mine with them. I saw *him* walking among them. The sight maddened me; my blood burned; I leaped on him; with two blows I laid him dead at my feet. I covered him with earth and strewed leaves over the place. Then I went to *her* and told her what I had done, and urged her to fly with me. She answered only with tears. I reminded her of all she had suffered, and told her I had done only what was just. I urged her again to fly. She only wept the more, and bade me go. My heart was heavy but my eyes were dry.

"'It is well,' I said, 'I will go alone to the desert. None but the wild beasts of the wilderness will be with me. The seekers of blood will follow on my trail; they may come on me while I am asleep and slay me, but you will be safe. I will go alone.'

"I turned to go. She sprang after me. 'No,' she cried, 'you shall not go alone. Wherever you go I will go: you shall never part from me.'

"While we were talking, one who had seen me slay the chief and had roused the camp, came with others. We heard their steps approaching the door, and knew that death came with them. We escaped at the back of the lodge, but they saw us and their arrows flew. She fell, and I caught her in my arms and fled into the wood. When we were safe I looked at her I carried, and she was dead. An arrow had 110 pierced her heart. I buried her that night beneath a heap of stones, and fled to the Cayuses. That is my story."

"What will you do now?" asked Cecil, deeply touched.

"I shall live a man's life. I shall hunt and go on the war-trail, and say strong words in the council. And when my life is ended, when the sunset and the night come to me and I go forth into the darkness, I know I shall find her I love waiting for me beside the death-trail that leads to the spirit-land."

The tears came into Cecil's eyes.

"I too have known sorrow," he said, "and like you I am a wanderer from my own people. We are going together into an unknown land, knowing not what may befall us. Let us be friends."

And he held out his hand. The Indian took it,—awkwardly, as an Indian always takes the hand of a white man, but warmly, heartily.

"We are brothers," he said simply. And as Cecil rode on with the wild troop into the unknown world before him, he felt that there was one beside him who would be faithful, no matter what befell.

The long day wore on; the sun rose to the zenith and sunk, and still the Indians pushed forward. It was a long, forced march, and Cecil was terribly fatigued when at last one of the Indians told him that they were near a big river where they would camp for the night.

"One sun more," said the Indian, pointing to the sun now sinking in the west, "and you will see the Bridge of the Gods."

The news re-animated Cecil, and he hurried on. A 111 shout rose from the Indians in advance. He saw the head of the long train of horses and riders pause and look downward and the Indians at the rear gallop forward. Cecil and his friend followed and joined them.

"The river! the river!" cried the Indians, as they rode up. The scene below was one of gloomy but magnificent beauty. Beneath them opened an immense canyon, stupendous even in that land of canyons,—the great canyon of the Columbia. The walls were brown, destitute of verdure, sinking downward from their feet in yawning precipices or steep slopes. At the bottom, more than a thousand feet below, wound a wide blue river, the gathered waters of half a continent. Beneath them, the river plunged over a long low precipice with a roar that filled the canyon for miles. Farther on, the flat banks encroached upon the stream till it seemed narrowed to a silver thread among the jutting rocks. Still farther, it widened again, swept grandly around a bend in the distance, and passed from sight.

"*Tuum, tuum*," said the Indians to Cecil, in tones that imitated the roar of the cataract. It was the "Tum" of Lewis and Clark, the "Tumwater" of more recent times; and the place below, where the compressed river wound like a silver thread among the flat black rocks, was the far-famed Dalles of the Columbia. It was superb, and yet there was something profoundly lonely and desolate about it,— the majestic river flowing on forever among barren rocks and crags, shut in by mountain and desert, wrapped in an awful solitude where from age to age scarce a sound was heard save the cry of wild beasts or wilder men.

112

"It is the very river of death and of desolation," thought Cecil. "It looks lonely, forsaken, as if no eye had beheld it from the day of creation until now."

Looking again at the falls, he saw, what he had not before noticed, a large camp of Indians on the side nearest them. Glancing across the river, he descried on a knoll on the opposite bank—what? Houses! He could not believe his eyes; could it be possible? Yes, they certainly were long, low houses, roofed as the white man roofs his. A sudden wild hope thrilled him; his brain grew dizzy. He turned to one of the Indians.

"Who built those houses?" he exclaimed; "white men like me?"

The other shook his head.

"No, Indians."

Cecil's heart died within him. "After all," he murmured, "it was absurd to expect to find a settlement of white men here. How could I think that any but Indians had built those houses?"

Still, as they descended the steep zigzag pathway leading down to the river, he could not help gazing again and again at the buildings that so reminded him of home.

It was Wishram, the ancient village of the falls, whose brave and insolent inhabitants, more than a century later, were the dread of the early explorers and fur traders of the Columbia. It was built at the last and highest fishery on the Columbia, for the salmon could not at that time ascend the river above the falls. All the wandering tribes of the Upper Columbia came there to fish or to buy salmon of the Wishram fishers. There too the Indians of the Lower 113 Columbia and the Willamette met them, and bartered the *hiagua* shells, the dried berries, and *wappatto* of their country for the bear claws and buffalo robes of the interior. It was a rendezvous where buying, selling, gambling, dancing, feasting took the place of war and the chase; though the ever burning enmities of the tribes sometimes flamed into deadly feuds and the fair-ground not infrequently became a field of battle.

The houses of Wishram were built of logs, the walls low, the lower half being below the surface of the ground, so that they were virtually half cellar. At a distance, the log walls and arched roofs gave them very much the appearance of a frontier town of the whites.

As they descended to the river-side, Cecil looked again and again at the village, so different from the skin or bark lodges of the Rocky Mountain tribes he had been with so long. But the broad and sweeping river flowed between, and his gaze told him little more than his first glance had done.

They were now approaching the camp. Some of the younger braves at the head of the Cayuse train dashed toward it, yelling and whooping in the wildest manner. Through the encampment rang an answering shout.

"The Cayuses! the Cayuses! and the white medicine-man!"

The news spread like wildfire, and men came running from all directions to greet the latest arrivals. It was a scene of abject squalor that met Cecil's eyes as he rode with the others into the camp. Never had he seen among the Indian races aught so degraded as those Columbia River tribes.

114

The air was putrid with decaying fish; the very skins and mats that covered the lodge-poles were black with rancid salmon and filth. Many of the men were nude; most of the women wore only a short garment of skin or woven cedar bark about the waist, falling scarcely to the knees. The heads of many had been artificially flattened; their faces were brutal; their teeth worn to the gums with eating sanded salmon; and here and there bleared and unsightly eyes showed the terrible prevalence of ophthalmia. Salmon were drying in the sun on platforms raised above the reach of dogs. Half-starved horses whose raw and bleeding mouths showed the effect of the hair-rope bridles, and whose projecting ribs showed their principal nutriment to be sage-brush and whip-lash, were picketed among the lodges. Cayote-like dogs and unclad children, shrill and impish, ran riot, fighting together for half-dried, half-decayed pieces of salmon. Prevailing over everything was the stench which is unique and unparalleled among the stenches of the earth,—the stench of an Indian camp at a Columbia fishery.[6]

Perhaps ten of the petty inland tribes had assembled there as their starting-point for the great council at Wappatto Island. All had heard rumors of the white man who had appeared among the tribes to the south saying that the Great Spirit had sent him to warn the Indians to become better, and all were anxious to see him. They pointed him out to one another as he rode up,—the man of graceful presence and delicate build; they thronged around him, naked 115 men and half-clad women, squalid, fierce as wild beasts, and gazed wonderingly.

"It is he, the white man," they whispered among themselves. "See the long beard." "See the white hands." "Stand back, the Great Spirit sent him; he is strong *tomanowos*; beware his anger."

Now the horses were unpacked and the lodges pitched, under the eyes of the larger part of the encampment, who watched everything with insatiable curiosity, and stole all that they could lay their hands on. Especially did they hang on every motion of Cecil; and he sank very much in their estimation when they found that he helped his servant, the old Indian woman, put up his lodge.

"Ugh, he does squaw's work," was the ungracious comment. After awhile, when the lodge was up and Cecil lay weary and exhausted upon his mat within it, a messenger entered and told him that the Indians were all collected near the river bank and wished him to come and give them the "talk" he had brought from the Great Spirit.

Worn as he was, Cecil arose and went. It was in the interval between sunset and dark. The sun still shone on the cliffs above the great canyon, but in the spaces below the shadows were deepening. On the flat rocks near the bank of the river, and close by the falls of Tumwater, the Indians were gathered to the number of several hundred, awaiting him,—some squatting, Indian fashion, on the ground, others standing upright, looking taller than human in the dusky light. Mingled with the debased tribes that made up the larger part of the gathering, Cecil saw here and there warriors of a bolder and superior race,—Yakimas 116 and Klickitats, clad in skins or wrapped in blankets woven of the wool of the mountain sheep.

Cecil stood before them and spoke, using the Willamette tongue, the language of common intercourse between the tribes, all of whom had different dialects. The audience listened in silence while he told them of the goodness and compassion of the Great Spirit; how it grieved him to see his children at war among themselves, and how he, Cecil, had been sent to warn them to forsake their sins and live better lives. Long familiarity with the Indians had imparted to him somewhat of their manner of thinking and speaking; his language had become picturesque with Indian imagery, and his style of oratory had acquired a tinge of Indian gravity. But the intense and vivid spirituality that had ever been the charm of his eloquence was in it still. There was something in his words that for the moment, and unconsciously to them, lifted his hearers to a higher plane. When he closed there was upon them that vague remorse, that dim desire to be better, that indefinable wistfulness, which his earnest, tender words never failed to arouse in his hearers.

When he lifted his hands at the close of his "talk," and prayed that the Great Spirit might pity them, that he might take away from them the black and wicked heart of war and hate and give them the new heart of peace and love, the silence was almost breathless, broken only by the unceasing roar of the falls and the solemn pleading of the missionary's voice.

He left them and returned through the deepening shadows to his lodge. There he flung himself on the couch of furs the old Indian woman had spread for 117 him. Fatigued with the long ride of the day and the heavy draught his address had made on an overtaxed frame, he tried to sleep.

But he could not. The buildings of the town of Wishram across the river, so like the buildings of the white man, had awakened a thousand memories of home. Vivid pictures of his life in New England and in the cloisters of Magdalen came before his sleepless eyes. The longing for the refined and pleasant things that had filled his life rose strong and irrepressible within him. Such thoughts were never entirely absent from his mind, but at times they seemed to dominate him completely, driving him into a perfect fever of unrest and discontent. After tossing for hours on his couch, he arose and went out into the open air.

The stars were bright; the moon flooded the wide canyon with lustre; the towering walls rose dim and shadowy on either side of the river whose waters gleamed white in the moonlight; the solemn roar of the falls filled the silence of the night.

Around him was the barbarian encampment, with here and there a fire burning and a group of warriors talking beside it. He walked forth among the lodges. Some were silent, save for the heavy breathing of the sleepers; others were lighted up within, and he could hear the murmur of voices.

At one place he found around a large fire a crowd who were feasting, late as was the hour, and boasting of their exploits. He stood in the shadow a moment and listened. One of them concluded his tale by springing to his feet, advancing a few paces from the circle of firelight, and making a fierce speech to invisible 118 foes. Looking toward the land of the Shoshones, he denounced them with the utmost fury, dared them to face him, scorned them because they did not appear, and ended by shaking his tomahawk in their direction, amid the applause of his comrades.

Cecil passed on and reached the outer limit of the camp. There, amid some large bowlders, he almost stumbled on a band of Indians engaged in some grisly ceremony. He saw them, however, in time to escape observation and screen himself behind one of the rocks.

One of the Indians held a rattlesnake pinned to the ground with a forked stick. Another held out a piece of liver to the snake and was provoking him to bite it. Again and again the snake, quivering with fury and rattling savagely, plunged his fangs into the liver. Several Indians stood looking on, with arrows in their hands. At length, when the meat was thoroughly impregnated with the virus, the snake was released and allowed to crawl away. Then they all dipped the points of their arrows in the poisoned liver,[7] carefully marking the shaft of each in order to distinguish it from those not poisoned. None of them saw Cecil, and he left without being discovered.

Why did they wish to go to the council with poisoned arrows?

Further on, among the rocks and remote from the camp, he saw a great light and heard a loud hallooing. He went cautiously toward it. He found a large fire in an open space, and perhaps thirty savages, stripped 119 and painted, dancing around it, brandishing their weapons and chanting a kind of war-chant. On every face, as the firelight fell on it, was mad ferocity and lust of war. Near them lay the freshly killed body of a horse whose blood they had been drinking. Drunk with frenzy, drunk with blood, they danced and whirled in that wild saturnalia till Cecil grew dizzy with the sight.[8]

He made his way back to the camp and sought his lodge. He heard the wolves howling on the hills, and a dark presentiment of evil crept over him.

"It is not to council that these men are going, but to war," he murmured, as he threw himself on his couch. "God help me to be faithful, whatever comes! God help me to keep my life and my words filled with his spirit, so that these savage men may be drawn to him and made better, and my mission be fulfilled! I can never hope to see the face of white man again, but I can live and die faithful to the last."

So thinking, a sweet and restful peace came to him, and he fell asleep. And even while he thought how impossible it was for him ever to reach the land of the white man again, an English exploring-ship lay at anchor at Yaquina Bay, only two days' ride distant; and on it were some who had known and loved him in times gone by, but who had long since thought him lost in the wilderness forever.

[5]

See Bonneville's Adventures, chapters xiii, and xlviii.

[6]

See Townsend's Narrative, pages 137, 138. Both Lewis and Clark and Ross Cox substantiate his description; indeed, very much the same thing can be seen at the Tumwater Fishery to-day.

[7]

See Bancroft's *Native Races*, article "Columbians." A bunch of arrows so poisoned is in the Museum of the Oregon State University at Eugene.

[8]

Irving's "Astoria," chap. xli.

CHAPTER III.

THE GREAT CAMP ON THE ISLAND.

Of different language, form and face,
A various race of men.

SCOTT.

"You say that we shall see the Bridge of the Gods to-day?" asked Cecil of the young Willamette runner the next morning. "Tell me about it; is it high?"

The young Willamette rose to his full height, arched his right hand above his eyes, looked skyward with a strained expression as if gazing up at an immense height, and emitted a prolonged "ah-h-h!"

That was all, but it was enough to bring the light to Cecil's eyes and a sudden triumphant gladness to his heart. At last he approached the land of his vision, at last he should find the bridge whose wraith had faded before him into the west eight years before!

The Cayuse band had started early that morning. The chief Snoqualmie was impatient of delay, and wished to be one of the earliest at the council; he wanted to signalize himself in the approaching struggle by his loyalty to Multnomah, whose daughter he was to marry and whom he was to succeed as war-chief.

The women were in advance, driving the pack-horses; Cecil rode behind them with the Shoshone renegade and the young Willamette runner; while Snoqualmie brought up the rear, looking sharply after 121 stragglers,—for some of his young men were very much inclined to linger at the rendezvous and indulge in a little gambling and horse-racing with the other bands, who were not to start till later in the day.

The young Willamette still rode the pretty little pony whose ears and tail he had so barbarously mutilated. It reeled under him from sheer weakness, so young was it and so worn by the journey of the day before. In vain did Cecil expostulate. With true Indian obtuseness and brutality, the Willamette refused to see why he should be merciful to a horse.

"Suppose he rode me, what would *he* care? Now I ride him, what do I care? Suppose he die, plenty more *hiagua* shells, plenty more horses."

After which logical answer he plied the whip harder than ever, making the pony keep up with the stronger and abler horses of the other riders. The long train of squaws and warriors wound on down the trail by the river-side. In a little while Wishram and Tumwater passed from sight. The wind began to blow; the ever drifting sand of the Columbia came sifting in their faces. They passed the Dalles of the Columbia; and the river that, as seen from the heights the evening before, wound like a silver thread among the rocks, was found to be a compressed torrent that rushed foaming along the narrow passage,—literally, as it has been described, "a river turned on edge."

There too they passed the camp of the Wascos, who were preparing to start, but suspended their preparations at the approach of the cavalcade and stood along the path eager to see the white man. Cecil noticed that as they descended the river the language of the local tribes became more gutteral, and 122 the custom of flattening the head prevailed more and more.[9]

Below, the scenery was less barren; the river entered the Cascade Range, and the steep banks, along which wound the trail, grew dark with pines, relieved here and there with brighter verdure. They saw bands of Indians on the opposite shore, descending the trail along that side on the way to the council. Many were on foot, though some horses were among them. They were Indians of the nine tribes of the Klickitat, and as yet had but few horses. A century later they owned thousands. Indian women never accompanied war-parties; and Cecil noticed that some of the bands were composed entirely of men, which gave them the appearance of going to war. It had an ominous and doubtful look.

At the Wau-coma (place of cottonwoods), the modern Hood River, they found the tribe that inhabited that beautiful valley already on the march, and the two bands mingled and went on together. The Wau-comas seemed to be peaceably inclined, for their women were with them.

A short distance below the Wau-coma, the young Willamette's horse, urged till it could go no farther, fell beneath him. The blood gushed from its nostrils; in a few moments it was dead. The Willamette extricated himself from it. "A bad horse, *cultus* [no good]!" he said, beating it with his whip. After venting his anger on it in that way, he strode forward on foot.

And now Cecil was all expectation, on the alert for the first sight of the bridge.

123

"Shall we see it soon?" he asked the young Willamette.

"When the sun is there, we shall see it," replied the Indian, pointing to the zenith. The sun still lacked several hours of noon, and Cecil had to restrain his impatience as best he could.

Just then an incident occurred that for the time effectually obliterated all thought of the bridge, and made him a powerful enemy where he least desired one.

At a narrow place in the trail, the loose horses that were being driven at the head of the column became frightened and ran back upon their drivers. In a moment, squaws, pack-horses, and ponies were all mingled together. The squaws tried in vain to restore order; it seemed as if there was going to be a general stampede. The men dashed up from the rear, Snoqualmie and Cecil among them. Cecil's old nurse happened to be in Snoqualmie's way. The horse she rode was slow and obstinate; and when she attempted to turn aside to let Snoqualmie pass he would not obey the rein, and the chief's way was blocked. To Snoqualmie an old Indian woman was little more than a dog, and he raised his whip and struck her across the face.

Like a flash, Cecil caught the chief's rein and lifted his own whip. An instant more, and the lash would have fallen across the Indian's face; but he remembered that he was a missionary, that he was violating his own precepts of forgiveness in the presence of those whom he hoped to convert.

The blow did not fall; he grappled with his anger and held it back; but Snoqualmie received from him a look of scorn so withering, that it seemed when 124 Cecil's flashing eyes met his own as if he had been struck, and he grasped his tomahawk. Cecil released the rein and turned away without a word. Snoqualmie seemed for a moment to deliberate within himself; then he let go his weapon and passed on. Order was restored and the march resumed.

"You are strong," said the Shoshone renegade to Cecil. He had seen the whole of the little drama. "You are strong; you held your anger down, but your eyes struck him as if he were a dog."

Cecil made no reply, but rode on thinking that he had made an enemy. He regretted what had happened; and yet, when he recalled the insult, his blood burned and he half regretted that the blow had not been given. So, absorbed in painful thought, he rode on, till a murmur passing down the line roused him.

"The bridge! The bridge!"

He looked up hastily, his whole frame responding to the cry. There it was before him, and only a short distance away,—a great natural bridge, a rugged ridge of stone, pierced with a wide arched tunnel through which the waters flowed, extending across the river. It was covered with stunted pine and underbrush growing in every nook and crevice; and on it were Indian horsemen with plumed hair and rude lances. It was the bridge of the Wauna, the Bridge of the Gods, the bridge he had seen in his vision eight years before.

For a moment his brain reeled, everything seemed shadowy and unreal, and he half expected to see the bridge melt, like the vision, into mist before his eyes.

Like one in a dream, he rode with the others to the place where the path turned abruptly and led 125 over the bridge to the northern bank of the Columbia. Like one in a dream he listened, while the young Willamette told him in a low tone that this bridge had been built by the gods when the world was young, that it was the *tomanowos* of the Willamettes, that while it stood they would be strongest of all the tribes, and that if it fell they would fall with it. As they crossed it, he noted how the great arch rung to his horse's hoofs; he noted the bushes growing low down to the tunnel's edge; he noted how majestic was the current as it swept into the vast dark opening below, how stately the trees on either bank. Then the trail turned down the river-bank again toward the Willamette, and the dense fir forest shut out the mysterious bridge from Cecil's backward gaze.

Solemnity and awe came to him. He had seen the bridge of his vision; he had in truth been divinely called to his work. He felt that the sight of the bridge was both the visible seal of God upon his mission and a sign that its accomplishment was close at hand. He bowed his head involuntarily, as in the presence of the Most High. He felt that he rode to his destiny, that for him all things converged and culminated at the great council.

They had not advanced far into the wood ere the whole train came to a sudden halt. Riding forward, Cecil found a band of horsemen awaiting them. They were Klickitats, mounted on good ponies; neither women nor pack-horses were with them; they were armed and painted, and their stern and menacing aspect was more like that of men who were on the war-trail than of men who were riding to a "peace-talk."

126

The Cayuses halted a short distance away. Snoqualmie rode forward and met the Klickitat chief in the space between the two bands. A few words passed, fierce and questioning on the part of the Klickitat, guarded and reserved on the part of the Cayuse. Then the Klickitat seemed to suggest something at which the Cayuse shook his head indignantly. The other instantly wheeled his horse, rode back to his band, and apparently reported what Snoqualmie had said; for they all set up a taunting shout, and after flinging derisive words and gestures at the Cayuses, turned around and dashed at full gallop down the trail, leaving the Cayuses covered with a cloud of dust.

And then Cecil knew that the spectacle meant war.

The air grew softer and more moist as they descended the western slope of the Cascade Range. The pines gave way to forests of fir, the underwood became denser, and ferns grew thick along the trail. It had rained the night before, and the boughs and bushes hung heavy with pendant drops. Now and then an Indian rider, brushing against some vine or maple or low swaying bough, brought down upon himself a drenching shower. The disgusted "ugh!" of the victim and the laughter of the others would bring a smile to even Cecil's lips.

And so approaching the sea, they entered the great, wooded, rainy valley of the lower Columbia. It was like a different world from the desert sands and prairies of the upper Columbia. It seemed as if they were entering a land of perpetual spring. They passed through groves of spreading oaks; they skirted lowlands purple with blooming *camas*; they crossed 127 prairies where the grass waved rank and high, and sunny banks where the strawberries were ripening in scarlet masses. And ever and anon they caught sight of a far snow peak lifted above the endless reach of forest, and through openings in the trees caught glimpses of the Columbia spreading wide and beautiful between densely wooded shores whose bending foliage was literally washed by the waters.

At length, as the sun was setting, they emerged from the wood upon a wide and level beach. Before them swept the Columbia, broader and grander than at any previous view, steadily widening as it neared the sea. Opposite them, another river, not as large as the Columbia, but still a great river, flowed into it.

"Willamette," said the young runner, pointing to this new river. "Wappatto Island," he added, indicating a magnificent prospect of wood and meadow that lay just below the mouth of the Willamette down along the Columbia. Cecil could not see the channel that separated it from the mainland on the other side, and to him it seemed, not an island, but a part of the opposite shore.

Around them on the beach were groups of Indians, representatives of various petty tribes who had not yet passed to the island of council. Horses were tethered to the driftwood strewed along the beach; packs and saddles were heaped on the banks awaiting the canoes that were to carry them over. Across the river, Cecil could see upon the island scattered bands of ponies feeding and many Indians passing to and fro. Innumerable lodges showed among the trees. The river was dotted with canoes. Never before had he beheld so large an encampment, not even among 128 the Six Nations or the Sioux. It seemed as if all the tribes of Puget Sound and the Columbia were there.

As they halted on the bank, a little canoe came skimming over the water like a bird. It bore a messenger from Multnomah, who had seen the Cayuses as soon as they emerged on the beach.

"Send your packs over in canoes, swim your horses, camp on the island," was the laconic message. Evidently, in view of the coming struggle, Multnomah wanted the loyal Cayuses close at hand.

In a little while the horses were stripped of their packs, which were heaped in the canoes that had followed the messenger, and the crossing began. A hair rope was put around the neck of a horse, and the end given to a man in a canoe. The canoe was then paddled out into the stream, and the horse partly pulled, partly pushed into the river. The others after much beating followed their leader; and in a little while a long line of half submerged horses and riders was struggling across the river, while the loaded canoes brought up the rear. The rapid current swept them downward, and they landed on the opposite bank at a point far below that from which they started.

On the bank of the Columbia, near Morgan's Lake, an old gnarled cottonwood still marks the ancient landing-place; and traces remain of the historic trail which led up from the river-bank into the interior of the island,—a trail traversed perhaps for centuries,—the great Indian road from the upper Columbia to the Willamette valley.

The bank was black with people crowding out to see the latest arrivals. It was a thronging multitude 129 of dusky faces and diverse costumes. The Nootka with his tattooed face was there, clad in his woollen blanket, his gigantic form pushing aside the short Chinook of the lower Columbia, with his crooked legs, his half-naked body glistening with grease, his slit nose and ears loaded with *hiagua* shells. Choppunish women, clad in garments of buckskin carefully whitened with clay, looked with scorn on the women of the Cowlitz and Clatsop tribes, whose only dress was a fringe of cedar bark hanging from the waist. The abject Siawash of Puget Sound, attired in a scanty patch-work of rabbit and woodrat skin, stood beside the lordly Yakima, who wore deerskin robe and leggins. And among them all, conscious of his supremacy, moved the keen and imperious Willamette.

They all gazed wonderingly at Cecil, "the white man," the "long beard," the "man that came from the Great Spirit," the *"shaman* of strong magic,"—for rumors of Cecil and his mission had spread from tribe to tribe.

Though accustomed to savage sights, this seemed to Cecil the most savage of all. Flat heads and round heads; faces scarred, tattooed, and painted; faces as wild as beasts'; faces proud and haughty, degraded and debased; hair cut close to the head, tangled, matted, clogged with filth, carefully smoothed and braided,—every phase of barbarism in its most bloodthirsty ferocity, its most abject squalor, met his glance as he looked around him. It seemed like some wild phantasmagoria, some weird and wondrous dream; and the discord of tongues, the confusion of dialects, completed the bewildering scene.

Through the surging crowd they found their 130 way to the place where their lodges were to be pitched.

On the morrow the great council was to begin,—the council that to the passions of that mob of savages might be as the torch to dry brushwood. On the morrow Multnomah would try and would condemn to death a rebel chief in the presence of the very ones who were in secret league with him; and the setting sun would see the Willamette power supreme and undisputed, or the confederacy would be broken forever in the death-grapple of the tribes.

[9]

Lewis and Clark. See also Irving's "Astoria."

131

CHAPTER IV.

AN INDIAN TRIAL.

Like flame within the naked hand
His body bore his burning heart.

DANTE ROSSETTI.

Wappatto Island had seen many gatherings of the tribes, but never before had it seen so large an assembly as on the opening day of the council. The great cottonwoods of the council-grove waved over an audience of sachems and warriors the like of which the oldest living Indian could not remember.

No weapons were to be seen, for Multnomah had commanded that all arms be left that day in the lodges. But the dissatisfied Indians had come with weapons hidden under their robes of deer or wolf skin, which no one should have known better than Multnomah. Had he taken any precautions against surprise? Evidently not. A large body of Willamette warriors, muffled in their blankets, lounged carelessly around the grove, with not a weapon visible among them; behind them thronged the vast and motley assemblage of doubtful allies; and back of them, on the outskirts of the crowd, were the faithful Cayuses, unarmed like the Willamettes. Had Multnomah's wonderful astuteness failed him now when it was never needed more?

132

He was on the council-seat, a stone covered with furs; the Willamette sachems sat in their places facing him; and mats were spread for the chiefs of the tributaries. On a bearskin before the stern war-chief lay a peace-pipe and a tomahawk; and to the Indians, accustomed to signs and symbols, the two had a grim significance.

One by one the chiefs entered the circle and took their seats on the mats provided for them. Those who were friendly to Multnomah first laid presents before him; those who were not, took their places without offering him either gift or salutation. Multnomah, however, seemed unconscious of any neglect.

The chief of a Klamath tribe offered him a brilliantly dyed blanket; another, a finely fringed quiver, full of arrows; another, a long and massive string of *hiagua* shells. Each laid his gift before Multnomah and took his seat in silence.

The chief of the Chopponish presented him with a fine horse, the best belonging to his tribe. Multnomah accepted it, and a slave led it away. Then came Snoqualmie, bringing with him Cecil Grey. The chief's hour of vengeance was at hand.

"Behold the white man from the land where the sun rises, the white *shaman* of whom all the tribes have heard. He is thine. Let him be the white slave of Multnomah. All the chiefs have slaves, but who will have a white slave like Multnomah?"

Cecil saw the abyss of slavery yawning before him, and grew pale to the lips. His heart sank within him; then the resolute purpose that never failed him in time of peril returned; he lifted his head and met Multnomah's gaze with dignity. The war-chief 133 bent on him the glance which read men to the heart.

"The white stranger has been a chief among his own people," he said to Cecil, more in the manner of one asserting a fact than asking a question.

"I have often spoken to my people in the gatherings to hear the word of the Great Spirit."

Again the keen, inscrutable gaze of the great chief seemed to probe his being to its core; again the calm, grave stranger met it without shrinking. The instinct, so common among savage races, of in some way *knowing* what a man is, of intuitively grasping his true merit, was possessed by Multnomah in a large degree; and the royalty in his nature instinctively recognized the royalty in Cecil's.

"The white guest who comes into the land of Multnomah shall be to him as a guest; the chief should still be chief in any land. White stranger, Multnomah gives you welcome; sit down among the chiefs."

Cecil took his place among them with all the composure he could command, well knowing that he who would be influential among the Indians must seem to be unmoved by any change of fortune. He felt, however, not only the joy of personal deliverance, but mingled with it came the glad, triumphant thought that he had now a voice in the deliberations of the chiefs; it was a grand door opened for Indian evangelization. As for Snoqualmie, his face was as impassive as granite. One would have said that Cecil's victory was to him a matter of no moment at all. But under the guise of indifference his anger burned fierce and deadly,—not against Multnomah but against Cecil.

134

The last chief had taken his place in the council. There was a long, ceremonious pause. Then Multnomah arose. He looked over the council, upon the stern faces of the Willamettes and the loyal tributaries, upon the sullen faces of the malcontents, upon the fierce and lowering multitude beyond. Over the throng he looked, and felt as one feels who stands on the brink of a volcano; yet his strong voice never rang stronger, the grand old chief never looked more a chief than then.

"He is every inch a king," thought Cecil. The chief spoke in the common Willamette language, at that time the medium of intercourse between the tribes as the Chinook is now. The royal tongue was not used in a mixed council.

"Warriors and chiefs, Multnomah gives you welcome. He spreads the buffalo-robe." He made the Indian gesture of welcome, opening his hands to them with a backward and downward gesture, as of one spreading a robe. "To the warriors Multnomah says, 'The grass upon my prairies is green for your horses; behold the wood, the water, the game; they are yours.' To the chiefs he says, 'The mat is spread for you in my own lodge and the meat is cooked.' The hearts of the Willamettes change not as the winters go by, and your welcome is the same as of old. Word came to us that the tribes were angry and had spoken bitter things against the Willamettes; yes, that they longed for the confederacy to be broken and the old days to come again when tribe was divided against tribe and the Shoshones and Spokanes trampled upon you all. But Multnomah trusted his allies; for had they not smoked the peace-pipe with him and gone 135 with him on the war-trail? So he stopped his ears and would not listen, but let those rumors go past him like thistle-down upon the wind.

"Warriors, Multnomah has shown his heart. What say you? Shall the peace-pipe be lighted and the talk begin?"

He resumed his seat. All eyes turned to where the peace-pipe and the tomahawk lay side by side before the council. Multnomah seemed waiting for them to choose between the two.

Then Snoqualmie, the bravest and most loyal of the tributaries, spoke.

"Let the peace-pipe be lighted; we come not for strife, but to be knit together."

The angry malcontents in the council only frowned and drew their blankets closer around them. Tohomish the seer, as the oldest chief and most renowned medicine-man present, came forward and lighted the pipe,—a long, thin piece of carving in black stone, the workmanship of the Nootkas or Hydahs, who made the more elaborate pipes used by the Indians of the Columbia River.

Muttering some mystical incantation, he waved it to the east and the west, to the north and the south; and when the charm was complete, gave it to Multnomah, who smoked it and passed it to Snoqualmie. From chief to chief it circled around the whole council, but among them were those who sat with eyes fixed moodily on the ground and would not so much as touch or look at it. As the pipe passed round there was a subdued murmur and movement in the multitude, a low threatening clamor, as yet held in check by awe of Multnomah and dread 136 of the Willamette warriors. But the war-chief seemed unconscious that any had refused the pipe. He now arose and said,—

"The pipe is smoked. Are not our hearts as one? Is there not perfect trust between us? Now let us talk. First of all, Multnomah desires wise words from his brethren. Last winter one of the tribes rose up against Multnomah, saying that he should no longer be elder brother and war-chief of the tribes. But the rebels were beaten and all of them slain save the chief, who was reserved to be tried before you. You in your wisdom shall decide what shall be done with the warrior who has rebelled against his chief and stained his hands with the blood of his brethren."

Two Willamette braves then entered the circle, bringing with them one whose hands were tied behind him, whose form was emaciated with hunger and disease, but whose carriage was erect and haughty. Behind came a squaw, following him into the very presence of Multnomah, as if resolved to share his fortunes to the last. It was his wife. She was instantly thrust back and driven with brutal blows from the council. But she lingered on the outskirts of the crowd, watching and waiting with mute, sullen fidelity the outcome of the trial. No one looked at her, no one cared for her; even her husband's sympathizers jostled the poor shrinking form aside,—for she was only a squaw, while he was a great brave.

He looked a great brave, standing there before Multnomah and the chiefs with a dignity in his mien that no reverse could crush, no torture could destroy. Haggard, starved, bound, his eyes gleamed deathless and unconquerable hate on council and war-chief alike. 137 There were dark and menacing looks among the malcontents; in the captive they saw personified their own loss of freedom and the hated domination of the Willamettes.

"Speak! You that were a chief, you whose people sleep in the dust,—what have you to say in your defence? The tribes are met together, and the chiefs sit here to listen and to judge."

The rebel sachem drew himself up proudly and fixed his flashing eyes on Multnomah.

"The tongue of Multnomah is a trap. I am brought not to be tried but to be condemned and slain, that the tribes may see it and be afraid. No one knows this better than Multnomah. Yet I will speak while I still live, and stand here in the sun; for I go out into the darkness, and the earth will cover my face, and my voice shall be heard no more among men.

"Why should the Willamettes rule the other tribes? Are they better than we? The Great Spirit gave us freedom, and who may make himself master and take it away?

"I was chief of a tribe; we dwelt in the land the Great Spirit gave our fathers; their bones were in it; it was ours. But the Willamettes said to us, 'We are your elder brethren, you must help us. Come, go with us to fight the Shoshones.' Our young men went, for the Willamettes were strong and we could not refuse them. Many were slain, and the women wailed despairingly. The Willamettes hunted on our hunting-grounds and dug the *camas* on our prairies, so that there was not enough for us; and when winter came, our children cried for food. Then the runners of the Willamettes came to us through the snow, 138 saying, 'Come and join the war-party that goes to fight the Bannocks.'

"But our hearts burned within us and we replied, 'Our hunting-grounds and our food you have taken; will you have our lives also? Go back and tell your chief that if we must fight, we will fight him and not the Bannocks.' Then the Willamettes came upon us and we fought them, for their tyranny was so heavy that we could not breathe under it and death had become better than life. But they were the stronger, and when did the heart of a Willamette feel pity? To-day I only am left, to say these words for my race.

"Who made the Willamettes masters over us? The Great Spirit gave us freedom, and none may take it away. Was it not well to fight? Yes; free my hands and give me back my people from the cairns and the death-huts, and we will fight again! I go to my death, but the words I have spoken will live. The hearts of those listening here will treasure them up; they will be told around the lodge-fires and repeated in the war-dance. The words I speak will go out among the tribes, and no man can destroy them. Yes, they go out words, but they will come back arrows and war in the day of vengeance when the tribes shall rise against the oppressor.

"I have spoken, my words are done."

He stood erect and motionless. The wrath and disdain passed from his features, and stoicism settled over them like a mask of stone. Multnomah's cold regard had not faltered a moment under the chief's invective. No denunciation could shake that iron self-control.

139

The rebellious chiefs interchanged meaning glances; the throng of malcontents outside the grove pressed closer upon the ring of Willamette warriors, who were still standing or squatting idly around it. More than one weapon could be seen among them in defiance of the war-chief's prohibition; and the presage of a terrible storm darkened on those grim, wild faces. The more peaceably disposed bands began to draw themselves apart. An ominous silence crept through the crowd as they felt the crisis approaching.

But Multnomah saw nothing, and the circle of Willamette warriors were stolidly indifferent.

"Can they not see that the tribes are on the verge of revolt?" thought Cecil, anxiously, fearing a bloody massacre.

"You have heard the words of the rebel. What have you to say? Let the white man speak first, as he was the last to join us."

Cecil rose and pictured in the common Willamette tongue, with which he had familiarized himself during his long stay with the Cayuses, the terrible results of disunion, the desolating consequences of war,—tribe clashing against tribe and their common enemies trampling on them all. Even those who were on the verge of insurrection listened reverently to the "white wizard," who had drawn wisdom from the Great Spirit; but it did not shake their purpose. Their own dreamers had talked with the Great Spirit too, in trance and vision, and had promised them victory over the Willamettes.

Tohomish followed; and Cecil, who had known some of the finest orators in Europe, listened in amazement to a voice the most musical he had ever 140 heard. He looked in wonder on the repulsive features that seemed so much at variance with those melodious intonations. Tohomish pleaded for union and for the death of the rebel. It seemed for a moment as if his soft, persuasive accents would win the day, but it was only for a moment; the spell was broken the instant he ceased. Then Snoqualmie spoke. One by one, the great sachems of the Willamettes gave their voices for death. Many of the friendly allies did not give their decision at all, but said to Multnomah,—

"You speak for us; your word shall be our word."

When the dissatisfied chiefs were asked for their counsel, the sullen reply was given,—

"I have no tongue to-day;" or "I do not know."

Multnomah seemed not to notice their answers. Only those who knew him best saw a gleam kindling in his eyes that told of a terrible vengeance drawing near. The captive waited passively, seeming neither to see nor hear.

At length all had spoken or had an opportunity to speak, and Multnomah rose to give the final decision. Beyond the circle of Willamettes, who were still indifferent and unconcerned, the discontented bands had thrown aside all concealment, and stood with bared weapons in their hands; all murmurs had ceased; there was a deathlike silence in the dense mob, which seemed gathering itself together for a forward rush,—the commencement of a fearful massacre.

Behind it were the friendly Cayuses, but not a weapon could be seen among them. The chief saw all; saw too that his enemies only waited for him to pronounce sentence upon the captive,—that that 141 was the preconcerted signal for attack. Now among some of the tribes sentence was pronounced not by word but by gesture; there was the gesture for acquittal, the gesture for condemnation.

Multnomah lifted his right hand. There was breathless suspense. What would it be? Fixing his eyes on the armed malcontents who were waiting to spring, he clinched his hand and made a downward gesture, as if striking a blow. It was the death-signal, the death-sentence.

In an instant a deafening shout rang through the grove, and the bloodthirsty mob surged forward to the massacre.

Then, so suddenly that it blended with and seemed a part of the same shout, the dreaded Willamette war-cry shook the earth. Quick as thought, the Willamettes who had been lounging so idly around the grove were on their feet, their blankets thrown aside, the weapons that had been concealed under them ready in their hands. A wall of indomitable warriors had leaped up around the grove. At the same moment, the Cayuses in the rear bared their weapons and shouted back the Willamette war-cry.

The rebels were staggered. The trap was sprung on them before they knew that there was a trap. Those in front shrank back from the iron warriors of Multnomah, those in the rear wavered before the fierce Cayuses. They paused, a swaying flood of humanity, caught between two lines of rock.

142

CHAPTER V.

SENTENCED TO THE WOLF-DEATH.

The other, great of soul, changed not
Countenance   stern.

DANTE.

In that momentary pause Multnomah did something that showed the cold disdainfulness of his character as nothing else could have done. He had given the death-sign; he had not yet told how or when death was to be inflicted. He gave the sentence *now*, as if in utter scorn of the battle-cloud that hung quivering, ready to burst.

"He would have torn the confederacy to pieces; let him be left bound in the wood of the wolves, and torn limb from limb by them as he would have rent the tribes asunder."

The two warriors who had brought the criminal into the council came forward, flung a covering over his head and face, and led him away. Perhaps no custom of the northwestern Indians was more sombre than this,—the covering of the culprit's eyes from the time of his sentence till his death. Never again were those eyes to behold the sun.

Then, and not till then, did Multnomah turn his gaze on the malcontents, who stood, desperate but hesitating, hemmed in by the Willamettes and the Cayuses.

143

"You have chosen the tomahawk instead of the peace-pipe. Shall Multnomah choose the tomahawk also? Know you not that Multnomah holds your lives in his hand, and that he can crush you like an eggshell if he chooses?"

The war-chief lifted his arm as he spoke, and slowly closed his fingers till his hand was clinched. The eyes of Willamette and tributary alike hung on those slowly closing fingers, with their own strained on their tomahawks. That was half the death-signal! Would he give the other half,—the downward gesture? The baffled rebels tasted all the bitterness of death in that agonizing suspense. They felt that their lives were literally in his grasp; and so the stern autocrat wished them to feel, for he knew it was a lesson they would never forget.

At length he spoke.

"Drop your weapons and Multnomah will forget what he has seen, and all will be well. Strike but a blow, and not one of you will ever go back over the trail to his home."

Then he turned to the chiefs, and there was that in his tones which told them to expect no mercy.

"How comes it that your braves lift their tomahawks against Multnomah in his own council and on his own land? Speak! chiefs must answer for their people."

There was sullen silence for a little time; then one of them muttered that it was the young men; their blood was hot, they were rash, and the chiefs could not control them.

"Can you not control your young men? Then you are not fit to be chiefs, and are chiefs no longer." 144 He gave a signal to certain of the Willamettes who had come up behind the rebellious leaders, as they stood confused and hesitating in the council. They were seized and their hands bound ere they could defend themselves; indeed, they made no effort to do so, but submitted doggedly.

"Take them down the Wauna in the sea-canoes and sell them as slaves to the Nootkas who hunt seal along the coast. Their people shall see their faces no more. Slaves in the ice-land of the North shall they live and die."

The swarthy cheeks of the captives grew ashen, and a shudder went through that trapped and surrounded mob of malcontents. Indian slavery was always terrible; but to be slaves to the brutal Indians of the north, starved, beaten, mutilated, chilled, and benumbed in a land of perpetual frost; to perish at last in the bleak snow and winter of almost arctic coasts,—that was a fate worse than the torture-stake.

Dreadful as it was, not a chief asked for mercy. Silently they went with their captors out of the grove and down the bank to the river's edge. A large sea-canoe, manned by Chinook paddlers, was floating at the beach. They quickly embarked, the paddles dipped, the canoe glided out into the current and down the stream. In a few moments the cottonwood along the river's edge hid it from sight, and the rebels were forever beyond the hope of rescue.

Swift and merciless had the vengeance of Multnomah fallen, and the insurrection had been crushed at a blow. It had taken but a moment, and it had all passed under the eyes of the malcontents, who were still surrounded by the loyal warriors.

145

When the canoe had disappeared and the gaze of that startled and awed multitude came back to Multnomah, he made a gesture of dismissal. The lines drew aside and the rebels were free.

While they were still bewildered and uncertain what to do, Multnomah instantly and with consummate address called the attention of the council to other things, thereby apparently assuming that the trouble was ended and giving the malcontents to understand that no further punishment was intended. Sullenly, reluctantly, they seemed to accept the situation, and no further indications of revolt were seen that day.

Popular young men, the bravest of their several tribes, were appointed by Multnomah to fill the vacant chieftainships; and that did much toward allaying the discontent. Moreover, some troubles between different tribes of the confederacy, which had been referred to him for arbitration, were decided with rare sagacity. At length the council ended for the day, the star of the Willamettes still in the ascendant, the revolt seemingly subdued.

So the first great crisis passed.

———

That evening a little band of Willamette warriors led the rebel sachem, still bound and blindfolded, down to the river's bank, where a canoe lay waiting them. His wife followed and tried to enter it with him, as if determined to share his fortunes to the very last; but the guard thrust her rudely away, and started the canoe. As it moved away she caught the prow wildly, despairingly, as if she could not let her warrior go. One of the guards struck her hands 146 brutally with his paddle, and she released her hold. The boat glided out into the river. Not a word of farewell had passed between the condemned man and his wife, for each disdained to show emotion in the presence of the enemy. She remained on the bank looking after him, mute and despondent,—a forlorn creature clothed in rags and emaciated with hunger, an outcast from all the tribes. She might have been regarded as a symbolic figure representing woman among the Indians, as she stood there with her bruised hands, throbbing with pain where the cruel blow had fallen, hanging, in sullen scorn of pain, uncared for by her side. So she stood watching the canoe glide down the river, till it was swallowed up in the gathering shadows of evening.

The canoe dropped down the river to a lonely point on the northern shore, a place much frequented by wolves. There, many miles below the encampment on the island, they disembarked and took the captive into the wood. He walked among them with a firm and even tread; there was no sign of flinching, though he must have known that his hour was close at hand. They bound him prostrate at the foot of an oak, tying him to the hard, tough roots that ran over the ground like a network, and from which the earth had been washed away, so that thongs could be passed around them.

Head and foot they bound him, drawing the rawhide thongs so tight that they sank into the flesh, and knotting them, till no effort possible to him could have disentangled him. It was on his lips to ask them to leave one arm free, so that he might at least die fighting, though it were with but one naked hand. 147 But he hated them too much to ask even that small favor, and so submitted in disdainful silence.

The warriors all went back to the canoe, except one, an old hunter, famed for his skill in imitating every cry of bird or beast. Standing beside the bound and prostrate man, he sent forth into the forest the cry of a wolf. It rang in a thousand echoes and died away, evoking no response. He listened a moment with bated breath, but could hear nothing but the deep heart-beat of the man at his feet. Another cry, with its myriad echoes, was followed by the oppressive sense of stillness that succeeds an outcry in a lonely wood. Then came a faint, a far-off sound, the answer of a wolf to a supposed mate. The Indian replied, and the answer sounded nearer; then another blended with it, as the pack began to gather. Again the Indian gave the cry, wild and wolfish, as only a barbarian, half-beast by virtue of his own nature, could have uttered it. An awful chorus of barking and howling burst through the forest as the wolves came on, eager for blood.

The Indian turned and rejoined his comrades at the canoe. They pushed out into the river, but held the boat in the current by an occasional paddle-stroke, and waited listening. Back at the foot of the tree the captive strained every nerve and muscle in one mighty effort to break the cords that bound him; but it was useless, and he lay back with set teeth and rigid muscles, while his eyes sought in vain through their thick covering to see the approach of his foes. Presently a fierce outburst of howls and snarls told the listeners that the wolves had found their prey. They lingered and listened a little longer, but no sound or 148 cry was heard to tell of the last agony under those rending fangs; the chief died in silence. Then the paddles were dipped again in the water, and the canoe glided up the river to the camp.

When they reached the shore they found the rebel's wife awaiting them in the place where they had left her. She asked no questions; she only came close and looked at their faces in the dusk, and read there the thing she sought to know. Then she went silently away. In a little while the Indian wail for the dead was sounding through the forest.

"What is that?" asked the groups around the camp fires.

"The rebel chief's wife wailing the death-wail for her husband," was the low reply; and in that way the tribes knew that the sentence had been carried out. Many bands were there, of many languages, but all knew what that death-wail meant the instant it fell upon their ears. Multnomah heard it as he sat in council with his chiefs, and there was something in it that shook even his iron heart; for all the wilder, more superstitious elements of the Indians thrilled to two things,— the war-cry and the death-wail. He dismissed his chiefs and went to his lodge. On the way he encountered Tohomish, lurking, as was his wont, under the shadow of the trees.

"What think you now, Tohomish, you who love darkness and shadow, what think you? Is not the arm of the Willamette strong? Has it not put down revolt to-day, and held the tribes together?"

The Pine Voice looked at him sorrowfully.

"The vision I told in the council has come back to me again. The cry of woe I heard far off then is 149 nearer now, and the throng on the death-trail passes thicker and swifter. That which covered their faces is lifted, and their faces are the faces of Willamettes, and Multnomah is among them. The time is close at hand."

"Say this before our enemies, and, strong *tomanowos* though you are, you die!" said the chief, laying his hand on his tomahawk. But the seer was gone, and Multnomah stood alone among the trees.

Every evening at dusk, the widow of the rebel sachem went out into the woods near the camp and wailed her dead. Every night that wild, desolate lament was lifted and rang through the great encampment,—a cry that was accusation, defiance, and lament; and even Multnomah dared not silence her, for among the Indians a woman lamenting her dead was sacred. So, while Multnomah labored and plotted for union by day, that mournful cry raised the spirit of wrath and rebellion by night. And thus the dead liberator was half avenged.

BOOK IV.

THE LOVE TALE.

CHAPTER I.

THE INDIAN TOWN.

The bare ground with hoarie mosse bestrowed
Must be their bed, their pillow was unsowed
And the frutes of the forrest was their feast.

The Faërie Queene.

Never before had there come to Cecil so grand an opportunity for disseminating gospel truth. The work of half a lifetime might be done in a few days.

"The tribes are all gathered together in one encampment, and I can talk with them all, tell them of God, of the beauty of heaven and of the only Way. Then, when they disperse, they will carry my teaching in every direction, and so it will be scattered throughout all this wild land."

This was the thought that came to Cecil when he awoke on the morning after the trial. Now was the time to work! Now was the time for every element of argument, persuasion, and enthusiasm to be exerted to the utmost.

Earnestly did he pray that morning, kneeling in his lodge beside his couch of furs, that God would be with 152 and help him. And as he prayed, warm and glowing was the love and tenderness that filled his heart. When the day was a little more advanced, he entered upon his work. The camp was astir with life; nearly all had finished their morning meal, and the various employments and diversions of the day were begun. Each tribe or band had pitched its lodges apart, though not far from the others. It was not so much an encampment as a group of many encampments, and the whole made up a scattered town of huts and wigwams.

A precarious and uncertain quiet had succeeded the agitation of the day before. Multnomah's energy had awed the malcontents into temporary submission, and the different bands were mingling freely with one another; though here and there a chief or warrior looked on contemptuously, standing moodily apart, wrapped in his blanket. Now and then when a Willamette passed a group who were talking and gesticulating animatedly they would become silent all at once till the representative of the dreaded race was out of hearing, when a storm of indignant gutterals would burst forth; but there were no other indications of hostility.

Groups were strolling from place to place observing curiously the habits and customs of other tribes; the common Willamette tongue, precursor of the more modern Chinook jargon, furnishing a means of intercourse. Everywhere Cecil found talk, barter, diversion. It was a rude caricature of civilization, the picture of society in its infancy, the rough dramatization of that phase through which every race passes in its evolution from barbarism.

153

At one place, a hunter from the interior was bartering furs for *hiagua* shells to a native of the sea-coast. At another, a brave skilled in wood-work had his stock of bows and arrows spread out before him, and an admiring crowd were standing around looking on. But the taciturn brave sat coolly polishing and staining his arrows as if he were totally unconscious of spectators, until the magical word "buy" was mentioned, when he at once awoke to life and drove a bargain in bow and quiver *versus* dried berries and "ickters" that would have done credit to a Yankee.

At one place sat an old warrior from the upper Columbia, making arrow-heads, chipping off the little scales of flint with infinite patience, literally *wearing* the stone into the requisite shape. Beside him lay a small pack of flints brought from beyond the mountains, for such stone was rarely found along the lower Columbia. Squaws sat in front of their wigwams sewing mats,—carefully sorting the rushes, putting big ends with little ends, piercing each with a bodkin, and sewing them all together with a long bone needle threaded with buckskin or sinew. Others were weaving that water-tight wickerwork which was, perhaps, the highest art to which the Oregon Indians ever attained. Here a band of Indians were cooking, feasting, laughing, shouting around a huge sturgeon captured the night before. There a circle of gamblers were playing "hand,"—passing a small stick secretly from hand to hand and guessing whose hand contained it,—singing as they played that monotonous "ho-ha, ho-ha, ho-ha," which was the inseparable accompaniment of dancing, gambling, and horseback riding.

Among them all Cecil moved with the calm dignity 154 he had acquired from long intercourse with the Indians. Wherever he went there was silence and respect, for was he not the great white medicine-man? Gambling circles paused in the swift passage of the stick and the monotone of the chant to look and to comment; buyers and sellers stopped to gaze and to question; children who had been building miniature wigwams of sticks or floating bark canoes in the puddles, ran away at his approach and took shelter in the thickets, watching him with twinkling black eyes.

Wherever there was opportunity, he stopped and talked, scattering seed-thoughts in the dark minds of the Indians. Wherever he paused a crowd would gather; whenever he entered a wigwam a throng collected at the door.

Let us glance for a moment into the domestic life of the Indians as Cecil saw it that morning.

He enters one of the large bark huts of the Willamette Indians, a long, low building, capable of sheltering sixty or seventy persons. The part around the door is painted to represent a man's face, and the entrance is through the mouth. Within, he finds a spacious room perhaps eighty or a hundred feet long by twenty wide, with rows of rude bunks rising tier above tier on either side. In the centre are the stones and ashes of the hearth; above is an aperture in the roof for the escape of smoke; around the hearth mats are spread to sit upon;

the bare ground, hard and trodden, forms the only floor, and the roof is made of boards that have been split out with mallet and wedges.

Cecil enters and stands a moment in silence; then 155 the head of the house advances and welcomes him. The best mat is spread for him to sit upon; food is brought,—pounded fish, nuts, and berries, and a kind of bread made of roots cooked, crushed together, and cut in slices when cold. All this is served on a wooden platter, and he must eat whether hungry or not; for to refuse would be the grossest affront that could be offered a Willamette host, especially if it were presented by his own hands. The highest honor that a western Oregon Indian could do his guest was to wait on him instead of letting his squaw do it. The Indian host stands beside Cecil and says, in good-humored hospitality, "Eat, eat much," nor is he quite pleased if he thinks that his visitor slights the offered food. When the guest can be no longer persuaded to eat more, the food is removed, the platter is washed in water, and dried with a wisp of twisted grass; a small treasure of tobacco is produced from a little buckskin pocket and a part of it carefully mixed with dried leaves;[10] the pipe is filled and smoked. Then, and not till then, may the Indian host listen to the talk of the white man.

So it was in lodge after lodge; he must first eat, be it ever so little. Two centuries later, the Methodist and Congregational missionaries found themselves confronted with the same oppressive hospitality among the Rocky Mountain Indians.[11] Nay, they need not visit a wigwam; let them but stroll abroad through the village, and if they were popular and the camp was well supplied with buffalo-meat, messengers would come with appalling frequency, bearing the laconic 156 invitation, "Come and eat;" and the missionary must go, or give offence, even though he had already gone to half a dozen wigwams on the same errand. There is a grim humor in a missionary's eating fresh buffalo-meat in the cause of religion until he is like to burst, and yet heroically going forth to choke down a few mouthfuls more, lest he offend some dusky convert.

At one house Cecil witnessed a painful yet comical scene. The Willamettes were polygamists, each brave having as many wives as he was able to buy; and Cecil was in a lodge where the brother of the head man of that lodge brought home his second wife. At the entrance of the second wife, all gay in Indian finery, the first did not manifest the sisterly spirit proper for the occasion. After sitting awhile in sullen silence, she arose and began to kick the fire about, accompanying that performance with gutteral exclamations addressed to no one in particular; she struck the dog, which chanced to be in the way, sending it yelping from the wigwam; and then, having worked herself into a rage, began to scold her husband, who listened grimly but said nothing. At last she turned on her new-found sister, struck her, and began to lay rending hands on the finery that their mutual husband had given her. That was instantly resented; and in a few moments the squaws were rolling on the floor, biting, scratching, and pulling each other's hair with the fury of devils incarnate. The dogs, attracted by the tumult, ran in and began to bark at them; the Indians outside the hut gathered at the door, looking in and laughing; the husband contemplated them as they rolled fighting at his feet, and then looked at 157 Cecil. It was undoubtedly trying to Indian dignity but the warrior sustained his admirably. "Bad, very bad," was the only comment he allowed himself to make. Cecil took his leave, and the brave kept up his air of indifference until the white man had gone. Then he quietly selected a cudgel from the heap of fire-wood by the doorway, and in a short time peace reigned in the wigwam.

In a lodge not far away, Cecil witnessed another scene yet more barbarous than this. He found a little blind boy sitting on the ground near the fire, surrounded by a quantity of fish-bones which he had been picking. He was made a subject for the taunting jibes and laughter of a number of men and women squatting around him. His mother sat by in the most cruel apathy and unconcern, and only smiled when Cecil expressed commiseration for her unfortunate and peculiarly unhappy child. It had been neglected and seemed almost starved. Those around apparently took pleasure in tormenting it and rendering it miserable, and vied with each other in applying to it insulting and degrading epithets. The little articles that Cecil gave to it, in the hope that the Indians seeing him manifest an interest in it would treat it more tenderly, it put to its mouth eagerly; but not finding them eatable, it threw them aside in disgust. Cecil turned away sick at heart. Worn, already weary, this last sight was intolerable; and he went out into the woods, away from the camp.

But as he walked along he seemed to see the child again, so vividly had it impressed his imagination. It rose before him in the wood, when the noise of the camp lay far behind; it seemed to turn its sightless 158 eyes upon him and reach out its emaciated arms as if appealing for help.[12]

Out in the wood he came across an Indian sitting on a log, his face buried in his hands, his attitude indicating sickness or despondency. He looked up as Cecil approached. It was the young Willamette runner who had been his companion on the journey down the Columbia. His face was haggard; he was evidently very sick. The missionary stopped and tried to talk with him, but could evoke little response, except that he did not want to talk, and that he wanted to be left alone. He seemed so moody and irritable that Cecil thought it best to leave him. His experience was that talking with a sick Indian was very much like stirring up a wounded rattlesnake. So he left the runner and went on into the forest, seeking the solitude without which he could scarcely have lived amid the degrading barbarism around him. His spirit required frequent communion with God and Nature, else he would have died of weariness and sickness of heart.

Wandering listlessly, he went on further and further from the camp, never dreaming of what lay before him, or of the wild sweet destiny to which that dim Indian trail was leading him through the shadowy wood.

---

[10]

Lewis and Clark.

[11]

See Parkman's "Oregon Trail," also, Parker's work on Oregon.

[12]

See Townsend's Narrative, pages 182-183.

159

CHAPTER II.

THE WHITE WOMAN IN THE WOOD.

I seek a sail that never looms from out the purple
haze
At rosy dawn, or fading eve, or in the noontide's
blaze.

CELIA THAXTER.

Cecil walked listlessly on through the wood. He was worn out by the day's efforts, though it was as yet but the middle of the afternoon. There was a feeling of exhaustion in his lungs, a fluttering pain about his heart, the result of years of over-work upon a delicate frame. With this feeling of physical weakness came always the fear that his strength might give way ere his work was done. Nor was this all. In these times of depression, the longing to see again the faces of his friends, to have again the sweet graceful things of the life that was forever closed to him, rushed over him in a bitter flood.

The trail led him to the bank of the Columbia, some distance below the encampment. He looked out over the blue river sweeping majestically on, the white snow-peaks, the canyons deep in the shadows of afternoon, the dense forest beyond the river extending away to the unknown and silent North as far as his eyes could reach.

"It is wonderful, wonderful!" he thought. "But I would give it all to look upon one white face."

160

So musing, he passed on down the bank of the river. He was now perhaps two miles from the camp and seemingly in complete solitude. After a little the path turned away from the beach and led toward the interior. As he entered the woodland he came upon several Indian sentinels who lay, bow in hand, beside the path. They sprang up, as if to intercept his passage; but seeing that it was the white *shaman* whom Multnomah had honored, and who had sat at the council with the great sachems, they let him go on. Cecil indistinctly remembered having heard from some of the Indians that this part of the island was strictly guarded; he had forgotten why. So absorbed was he in his gloomy reflections that he did not stop to question the sentinels, but went on, not thinking that he might be treading on forbidden ground. By and by the path emerged from the wood upon a little prairie; the cottonwoods shut out the Indians from him, and he was again alone. The sunshine lay warm and golden on the little meadow, and he strolled forward mechanically, thinking how like it was to some of the sylvan lawns of his own New England forests. Again the shade of trees fell over the path. He looked up, his mind full of New England memories, and saw something that made his heart stand still. For there, not far from him, stood a girl clad in soft flowing drapery, the dress of a white woman. In Massachusetts a woman's dress would have been the last thing Cecil would have noticed. Now, so long accustomed to the Indian squaws' rough garments of skin or plaited bark, the sight of that graceful woven cloth sent through him an indescribable thrill.

161

He went on, his eager eyes drinking in the welcome sight, yet scarcely believing what he saw.

She had not yet observed him. The profile of her half-averted face was very sweet and feminine; her form was rounded, and her hair fell in long black ringlets to the shoulders. He was in the presence of a young and beautiful woman,—a white woman! All this he noted at a glance; noted, too, the drooping lashes, the wistful lines about the lips, the mournful expression that shadowed the beauty of her face.

Who was she? Where could she have come from?

She heard the approaching footsteps and turned toward him. Absolute bewilderment was on her face for a moment, and then it glowed with light and joy. Her dark, sad eyes sparkled. She was radiant, as if some great, long-looked for happiness had come to her. She came eagerly toward him, holding out her hands in impetuous welcome; saying something in a language he did not understand, but which he felt could not be Indian, so refined and pleasing were the tones.

He answered he knew not what, in his own tongue, and she paused perplexed. Then he spoke again, this time in Willamette.

She shrank back involuntarily.

"That language?" she replied in the same tongue, but with a tremor of disappointment in her voice. "I thought you were of my mother's race and spoke her language. But you *are* white, like her people?"

She had given him both her hands, and he stood holding them; looking down into her eager, lifted face, where a great hope and a great doubt in mingled light and shadow strove together.

162

"I am a white man. I came from a land far to the East. But who are you, and how came you here?"

She did not seem to hear the last words, only the first.

"No, no," she protested eagerly, "you came not from the East but from the West, the land across the sea that my mother came from in the ship that was wrecked." And she withdrew one hand and pointed toward the wooded range beyond which lay the Pacific.

He shook his head. "No, there are white people in those lands too, but I never saw them. I came from the East," he said, beginning to surmise that she must be an Asiatic. She drew away the hand that he still held in his, and her eyes filled with tears.

"I thought you were one of my mother's people," she murmured; and he felt that the pang of an exceeding disappointment was rilling her heart.

"Who are you?" he asked gently.

"The daughter of Multnomah."

Cecil remembered now what he had heard of the dead white wife of Multnomah, and of her daughter, who, it was understood among the tribes, was to be given to Snoqualmie. He noticed, too, for the first time the trace of the Indian in her expression, as the light faded from it and it settled back into the despondent look habitual to it. All that was chivalrous in his nature went out to the fair young creature; all his being responded to the sting of her disappointment.

"I am not what you hoped I was, but your face is 163 like the face of the women of my own land. Shall we not be friends?"

She looked up wistfully at the handsome and noble countenance above her, so different from the stolid visages she had known so long.

"Yes; you are not Indian."

In that one expression she unconsciously told Cecil how her sensitive nature shrank from the barbarism around her; how the tastes and aspirations she had inherited from her mother reached out for better and higher things.

In a little while they were seated on a grassy bank in the shade of the trees, talking together. She bade him tell her of his people. She listened intently; the bright, beautiful look came back as she heard the tale.

"They are kind to women, instead of making them mere burden-bearers; they have pleasant homes; they dwell in cities? Then they are like my mother's people."

"They are gentle, kind, humane. They have all the arts that light up life and make it beautiful,—not like the tribes of this grim, bloodstained land."

"*This* land!" Her face darkened and she lifted her hand in a quick, repelling gesture. "This land is a grave. The clouds lie black and heavy on the spirit that longs for the sunlight and cannot reach it." She turned to him again. "Go on, your words are music."

He continued, and she listened till the story of his country and his wanderings was done. When he ended, she drew a glad, deep breath; her eyes were sparkling with joy.

"I am content," she said, in a voice in which there 164 was a deep heart-thrill of happiness. "Since my mother died I have been alone, all alone; and I longed, oh so often, for some one who talked and felt as she did to come to me, and now you have come. I sat cold and shivering in the night a long time, but the light and warmth have come at last. Truly, Allah is good!"

"Allah!"

"Yes; he was my mother's God, as the Great Spirit is my father's."

"They are both names for the same All Father," replied Cecil. "They mean the same thing, even as the sun is called by many names by many tribes, yet there is but the one sun."

"Then I am glad. It is good to learn that both prayed to the one God, though they did not know it. But my mother taught me to use the name of Allah, and not the other. And while my father and the tribes call me by my Indian name, 'Wallulah,' she gave me another, a secret name, that I was never to forget."

"What is it?"

"I have never told it, but I will tell you, for you can understand."

And she gave him a singularly melodious name, of a character entirely different from any he had ever heard, but which he guessed to be Arabic or Hindu.

"It means, 'She who watches for the morning.' My mother told me never to forget it, and to remember that I was not to let myself grow to be like the Indians, but to pray to Allah, and to watch and hope, and that sometime the morning would come and I would be saved from the things around me. And 165 now you have come and the dawn comes with you."

Her glad, thankful glance met his; the latent grace and mobility of her nature, all roused and vivid under his influence, transfigured her face, making it delicately lovely. A great pang of longing surged through him.

"Oh," he thought, "had I not become a missionary, I might have met and loved some one like her! I might have filled my life with much that is now gone from it forever!"

For eight years he had seen only the faces of savage women and still more savage men; for eight years his life had been steeped in bitterness, and all that was tender or romantic in his nature had been cramped, as in iron fetters, by the coarseness and stolidity around him. Now, after all that dreary time, he met one who had the beauty and the refinement of his own race. Was it any wonder that her glance, the touch of her dress or hair, the soft tones of her voice, had for him an indescribable charm? Was it any wonder that his heart went out to her in a yearning tenderness that although not love was dangerously akin to it?

He was startled at the sweet and burning tumult of emotion she was kindling within him. What was he thinking of? He must shake these feelings off, or leave her. Leave her! The gloom of the savagery that awaited him at the camp grew tenfold blacker than ever. All the light earth held for him seemed gathered into the presence of this dark-eyed girl who sat talking so musically, so happily, by his side.

"I must go," he forced himself to say at length, "The sun is almost down."

166

"Must you go so soon?"

"I will come again if you wish."

"But you must not go yet; wait till the sun reaches the mountain-tops yonder. I want you to tell me more about your own land."

So he lingered and talked while the sun sank lower and lower in the west. It seemed to him that it had never gone down so fast before.

"I must go now," he said, rising as the sun's red disk sank behind the mountains.

"It is not late; see, the sun is shining yet on the brow of the snow mountains."

Both looked at the peaks that towered grandly in the light of the sunken sun while all the world below lay in shadow. Together they watched the mighty miracle of the afterglow on Mount Tacoma, the soft rose-flush that transfigured the mountain till it grew transparent, delicate, wonderful.

"That is what my life is now,—since you have brought the light to the 'watcher for the morning;'" and she looked up at him with a bright, trustful smile.

"Alas?" thought Cecil, "it is not the light of morning but of sunset."

Slowly the radiance faded, the rose tint passed; the mountain grew white and cold under their gaze, like the face of death. Wallulah shuddered as if it were a prophecy.

"You will come back to-morrow?" she said, looking at him with her large, appealing eyes.

"I will come," he said.

"It will seem long till your return, yet I have lived so many years waiting for that which has come at last that I have learned to be patient."

167

"Ask God to help you in your hours of loneliness and they will not seem so long and dark," said Cecil, whose soul was one tumultuous self-reproach that he had let the time go by without telling her more of God.

"Ah!" she said in a strange, wistful way, "I have prayed to him so much, but he could not fill *all* my heart. I wanted so to touch a hand and look on a face like my mother's. But God has sent you, and so I know he must be good."

They parted, and he went back to the camp.

"Is my mission a failure?" he thought, as he walked along, clinching his hands in furious anger with himself. "Why do I let a girl's beauty move me thus, and she the promised wife of another? How dare I think of aught beside the work God has sent me here to do? Oh, the shame and guilt of such weakness! I will be faithful. I will never look upon her face again!"

He emerged from the wood into the camp; its multitudinous sounds were all around him, and never had the coarseness and savagery of Indian life seemed so repellent as now, when he came back to it with his mind full of Wallulah's grace and loveliness. It was harsh discord after music.

Stripped and painted barbarians were hallooing, feasting, dancing; the whole camp was alive with boisterous hilarity, the result of a day of good fellowship. Mothers were calling their children in the dusk and young men were sportively answering, "Here I am, mother." Here and there, Indians who had been feasting all day lay like gorged anacondas beside the remnant of their meal; others, who had 168 been gambling, were talking loudly of the results of the game.

Through it all the white man walked with swift footsteps, looking neither to the right nor the left, till he gained his lodge. He flung himself on his bed and lay there, his fingers strained together convulsively, his nerves throbbing with pain; vainly struggling with regret, vainly repeating to himself that he cared nothing for love and home, that he had put all those things from him, that he was engrossed now only in his work.

"Never, never! It can never be."

<hr />

And the English exploring-ship in Yaquina Bay was to weigh anchor on the morrow, and sail up nearer along the unknown coast. The

Indians had all deserted the sea-board for the council. Would Cecil hear? Would any one see the sail and bring the news?

"I Will kill him!"

169

CHAPTER III.

CECIL AND THE WAR-CHIEF.

Children of the sun, with whom revenge is virtue.

YOUNG.

On the next day came the races, the great diversion of the Indians. Each tribe ran only one horse,—the best it had. There were thirty tribes or bands, each with its choicest racer on the track. The Puget Sound and lower Columbia Indians, being destitute of horses, were not represented. There had been races every day on a small scale, but they were only private trials of speed, while to-day was the great day of racing for all the tribes, the day when the head chiefs ran their horses.

The competition was close, but Snoqualmie the Cayuse won the day. He rode the fine black horse he had taken from the Bannock he had tortured to death. Multnomah and the chiefs were present, and the victory was won under the eyes of all the tribes. The haughty, insolent Cayuse felt that he had gained a splendid success. Only, as in the elation of victory his glance swept over the crowd, he met the sad, unapplauding gaze of Cecil, and it made his ever burning resentment grow hotter still.

"I hate that man," he thought. "I tried to thrust him down into slavery, and Multnomah made him a chief. My heart tells me that he is an enemy. I hate him. I will kill him."

170

"Poor Wallulah!" Cecil was thinking. "What a terrible future is before her as the wife of that inhuman torturer of men!"

And his sympathies went out to the lonely girl, the golden thread of whose life was to be interwoven with the bloodstained warp and woof of Snoqualmie's. But he tried hard not to think of her; he strove resolutely that day to absorb himself in his work, and the effort was not unsuccessful.

After the races were over, a solemn council was held in the grove and some important questions discussed and decided. Cecil took part, endeavoring in a quiet way to set before the chiefs a higher ideal of justice and mercy than their own. He was heard with grave attention, and saw that more than one chief seemed impressed by his words. Only Snoqualmie was sullen and inattentive, and Mishlah the Cougar was watchful and suspicious.

After the council was over Cecil went to his lodge. On the way he found the young Willamette runner sitting on a log by the path, looking even more woebegone than he had the day before. Cecil stopped to inquire how he was.

"*Cultus* [bad]," was grunted in response.

"Did you see the races?"

"Races bad. What do I care?"

"I hope you will be better soon."

"Yes, better or worse by and by. What do I care?"

"Can I do anything for you?"

"Yes."

"What is it?"

"Go."

171

And he dropped his hand upon his knees, doubled himself together, and refused to say another word. As Cecil turned to go he found Multnomah standing close by, watching him.

"Come," said the stern despot, briefly. "I want to talk with you."

He led the way back through the noisy encampment to the now deserted grove of council. Everything there was quiet and solitary;

the thick circle of trees hid them from the camp, though its various sounds floated faintly to them. They were quite alone. Multnomah seated himself on the stone covered with furs, that was his place in the council. Cecil remained standing before him, wondering what was on his mind. Was the war-chief aware of his interview with Wallulah? If so, what then? Multnomah fixed on him the gaze which few men met without shrinking.

"Tell me," he said, while it seemed to Cecil as if that eagle glance read every secret of his innermost heart, "tell me where your land is, and why you left it, and the reason for your coming among us. Keep no thought covered, for Multnomah will see it if you do."

Cecil's eye kindled, his cheek flushed. Wallulah was forgotten; his mission, and his mission only, was remembered. He stood before one who held over the many tribes of the Wauna the authority of a prince: if *he* could but be won for Christ, what vast results might follow!

He told it all,—the story of his home and his work, his call of God to go to the Indians, his long wanderings, the message he had to deliver, how it had been 172 received by some and rejected by many; now he was here, a messenger sent by the Great Spirit to tell the tribes of the Wauna the true way of life. He told it all, and never had he been so eloquent. It was a striking contrast, the grim Indian sitting there leaning on his bow, his sharp, treacherous gaze bent like a bird of prey on the delicately moulded man pleading before him.

He listened till Cecil began to talk of love and forgiveness as duties enjoined by the Great Spirit. Then he spoke abruptly.

"When you stood up in the council the day the bad chief was tried, and told of the weakness and the wars that would come if the confederacy was broken up, you talked wisely and like a great chief and warrior; now you talk like a woman. Love! forgiveness!" He repeated the words, looking at Cecil with a kind of wondering scorn, as if he could not comprehend such weakness in one who looked like a brave man. "War and hate are the life of the Indian. They are the strength of his heart. Take them away, and you drain the blood from his veins; you break his spirit; he becomes a squaw."

"But my people love and forgive, yet they are not squaws. They are brave and hardy in battle; their towns are great; their country is like a garden."

And he told Multnomah of the laws, the towns, the schools, the settled habits and industry of New England. The chief listened with growing impatience. At length he threw his arm up with an indescribable gesture of freedom, like a man rejecting a fetter.

"How can they breathe, shut in, bound down like that? How can they live, so tied and burdened?"

173

"Is not that better than tribe forever warring against tribe? Is it not better to live like men than to lurk in dens and feed on roots like beasts? Yet we will fight, too; the white man does not love war, but he will go to battle when his cause is just and war must be."

"So will the deer and the cayote fight when they can flee no longer. The Indian loves battle. He loves to seek out his enemy, to grapple with him, and to tread him down. That is a man's life!"

There was a wild grandeur in the chief's tone. All the tameless spirit of his race seemed to speak through him, the spirit that has met defeat and extermination rather than bow its neck to the yoke of civilization. Cecil realized that on the iron fibre of the war-chief's nature his pleading made no impression whatever, and his heart sank within him.

Again he tried to speak of the ways of peace, but the chief checked him impatiently.

"That is talk for squaws and old men. Multnomah does not understand it. Talk like a man, if you wish him to listen. Multnomah does not forgive; Multnomah wants no peace with his enemies. If they are weak he tramples on them and makes them slaves; if they are strong he fights them. When the Shoshones take from

Multnomah, he takes from them; if they give him war he gives them war; if they torture one Willamette at the stake, Multnomah stretches two Shoshones upon red-hot stones. Multnomah gives hate for hate and war for war. This is the law the Great Spirit has given the Indian. What law he has given the white man, Multnomah knows not nor cares!"

Baffled in his attempt, Cecil resorted to another 174 line of persuasion. He set before Multnomah the arts, the intelligence, the splendor of the white race.

"The Indian has his laws and customs, and that is well; but why not council with the white people, even as chiefs council together? Send an embassy to ask that wise white men be sent you, so that you may learn of their arts and laws; and what seems wise and good you can accept, what seems not so can be set aside. I know the ways that lead back to the land of the white man; I myself would lead the embassy."

It was a noble conception,—that of making a treaty between this magnificent Indian confederacy and New England for the purpose of introducing civilization and religion; and for a moment he lost sight of the insurmountable obstacles in the way.

"No," replied the chief, "neither alone nor as leader of a peace party will your feet ever tread again the path that leads back to the land of the white man. We want not upon our shoulders the burden of his arts and laws. We want not his teachers to tell us how to be women. If the white man wants us, let him find his way over the desert and through the mountains, and we will grapple with him and see which is the strongest."

So saying, the war-chief rose and left him.

"He says that I shall never be allowed to go back," thought Cecil, with a bitter consciousness of defeat. "Then my mission ends here in the land of the Bridge, even as I have so often dreamed that it would. So be it; I shall work the harder now that I see the end approaching. I shall gather the chiefs in my own lodge this evening and preach to them."

175

While he was forming his resolution, there came the recollection that Wallulah would look for him, would be expecting him to come to her.

"I cannot," he thought, though he yearned to go to her. "I cannot go; I must be faithful to my mission."

Many chiefs came that night to his lodge; among them, to his surprise, Tohomish the seer. Long and animated was Cecil's talk; beautiful and full of spiritual fervor were the words in which he pointed them to a better life. Tohomish was impassive, listening in his usual brooding way. The others seemed interested; but when he was done they all rose up and went away without a word,—all except the Shoshone renegade who had helped him bury the dead Bannock. He came to Cecil before leaving the lodge.

"Sometime," he said, "when it will be easier for me to be good than it is now, I will try to live the life you talked about to-night."

Then he turned and went out before Cecil could reply.

"There is one at least seeking to get nearer God," thought Cecil, joyfully. After awhile his enthusiasm faded away, and he remembered how anxiously Wallulah must have waited for him, and how bitterly she must have been disappointed. Her face, pale and stained with tears, rose plainly before him. A deep remorse filled his heart.

"Poor child! I am the first white person she has seen since her mother died; no wonder she longs for my presence! I must go to her to-morrow. After all, there is no danger of my caring for her. To me my work is all in all."

CHAPTER IV.

ARCHERY AND GAMBLING.

To gambling they are no less passionately addicted in the interior than on the coast.—BANCROFT: *Native Races.*

The next morning came the archery games. The best marksmen of each tribe contended together under the eyes of Multnomah, and Snoqualmie the Cayuse won the day.

These diversions were beginning to produce the result that the politic chief had intended they should. Better feeling was springing up. The spirit of discontent that had been rife was disappearing. Every day good-fellowship grew more and more between the Willamettes and their allies. Every day Snoqualmie the Cayuse became more popular among the tribes, and already he was second in influence to none but Multnomah himself.

The great war-chief had triumphed over every obstacle; and he waited now only for the last day of the council, when his daughter should be given to Snoqualmie and the chiefs should recognize him as the future head of the confederacy.

Knowing this, the sight of Snoqualmie's successful archery was almost intolerable to Cecil, and he turned away from the place where the games were held.

"I will seek the young Willamette who is sick," 177 he said to himself. "Then this evening I will go and visit Wallulah."

The thought sent the blood coursing warmly through his veins, but he chided himself for it. "It is but duty, I go to her only as a missionary," he repeated to himself over and over again.

He went to the lodge of the young Willamette and asked for him.

"He is not here," the father of the youth told him. "He is in the sweat-house. He is sick this morning, *hieu* sick."

And the old man emphasized the *hieu* [much], with a prolonged intonation and a comprehensive gesture as if the young man were very sick indeed. To the sweat-house went Cecil forthwith. He found it to be a little arched hut, made by sticking the ends of bent willow-wands into the ground and covering them over with skins, leaving only a small opening for entrance. When a sick person wished to take one of those "sweat baths" so common among the Indians, stones were heated red hot and put within the hut, and water was poured on them. The invalid, stripped to the skin, entered, the opening was closed behind him, and he was left to steam in the vapors.

When Cecil came up, the steam was pouring between the overlapping edges of the skins, and he could hear the young Willamette inside, chanting a low monotonous song, an endlessly repeated invocation to his *totem* to make him well. How he could sing or even breathe in that stifling atmosphere was a mystery to Cecil.

By and by the Willamette raised the flap that hung over the entrance and crawled out, hot, steaming, 178 perspiring at every pore. He rushed with unsteady footsteps down to the river, only a few yards away, and plunged into the cold water. After repeatedly immersing himself, he waded back to the shore and lay down to dry in the sun. The shock to his nervous system of plunging from a hot steam-bath into ice-cold water fresh from the snow peaks of the north had roused all his latent vitality. He had recovered enough to be sullen and resentful to Cecil when he came up; and after vainly trying to talk with or help him, the missionary left him.

It is characteristic of the Indian, perhaps of most half-animal races, that their moral conduct depends on physical feeling. Like the animal, they are good-humored, even sportive, when all is well; like the animal, they are sluggish and unreasoning in time of sickness.

Cecil went back to the camp. He found that the archery games were over, and that a great day of gambling had begun. He was astonished at the eagerness with which all the Indians flung themselves into it. Multnomah alone took no part, and Tohomish, visible only at the council, was not there. But with those two exceptions, chiefs, warriors, all flung themselves headlong into the game.

First, some of the leading chiefs played at "hand," and each tribe backed its chief. Furs, skins, weapons, all manner of Indian wealth was heaped in piles behind the gamblers, constituting the stakes; and they were divided among the tribes of the winners,—each player representing a tribe, and his winnings going, not to himself, but to his people. This rule applied, of course, only to the great public games; in private 179 games of "hand" each successful player kept his own spoils.

Amid the monotonous chant that always accompanied gambling, the two polished bits of bone (the winning one marked, the other not) were passed secretly from hand to hand. The bets were made as to who held the marked stick and in which hand, then a show of hands was made and the game was lost and won.

From "hand" they passed to *ahikia*, a game like that of dice, played with figured beaver teeth or disks of ivory, which were tossed up, everything depending on the combination of figures presented in their fall. It was played recklessly. The Indians were carried away by excitement. They bet anything and everything they had. Wealthy chiefs staked their all on the turn of the ivory disks, and some were beggared, some enriched. Cecil noticed in particular Mishlah the Cougar, chief of the Molallies. He was like a man intoxicated. His huge bestial face was all ablaze with excitement, his eyes were glowing like coals. He had scarcely enough intellect to understand the game, but enough combativeness to fling himself into it body and soul. He bet his horses and lost them; he bet his slaves and lost again; he bet his lodges, with their rude furnishings of mat and fur, and lost once more. Maddened, furious, like a lion in the toils, the desperate savage staked his wives and children on the throw of the *ahikia*, and they were swept from him into perpetual slavery.

Then he rose up and glared upon his opponents, with his tomahawk clinched in his hand,—as if feeling 180 dimly that he had been wronged, thirsting for vengeance, ready to strike, yet not knowing upon whom the blow should fall. There was death in his look, and the chiefs shrunk from him, when his eyes met Multnomah's, who was looking on; and the war-chief checked and awed him with his cold glance, as a tamer of beasts might subdue a rebellious tiger. Then the Molallie turned and went away, raging, desperate, a chief still, but a chief without lodge or wife or slave.

The sight was painful to Cecil, and he too went away while the game was at its height. Drawn by an influence that he could not resist, he took the trail that led down the bank of the river to the retreat of Wallulah.

181

CHAPTER V.

A DEAD QUEEN'S JEWELS.

For round about the walls yclothed were
With goodly arras of great maiesty,
Woven with golde and silke so close and nere
That the rich metall lurked privily.

The Faërie Queene.

He found the sentinels by the pathway half reluctant to let him pass, but they did not forbid him. Evidently it was only their awe of him as the "Great White Prophet," to whom Multnomah had added the dignity of an Indian sachem, that overcame their scruples. It was with a sense of doing wrong that he went on. "If Multnomah knew," he thought, "what would he do?" And brave as Cecil was, he shuddered, thinking how deadly the wrath of the war-chief would be, if he knew of these secret visits to his daughter.

"It is an abuse of hospitality; it is clandestine, wrong," he thought bitterly. "And yet she is lonely, she needs me, and I must go to her; but I will never go again."

Where he had met her before, he found her waiting for him now, a small, graceful figure, standing in the shadow of the wood. She heard his footsteps before he saw her, and the melancholy features were transfigured with joy. She stood hesitating a moment like 182 some shy creature of the forest, then sprang eagerly forward to meet him.

"I knew you were coming!" she cried rapturously. "I felt your approach long before I heard your footsteps."

"How is that?" said Cecil, holding her hands and looking down into her radiant eyes. Something of the wild Indian mysticism flashed in them as she replied:

"I cannot tell; I knew it! my spirit heard your steps long before my ears could catch the sound. But oh!" she cried in sudden transition, her face darkening, her eyes growing large and pathetic, "why did you not come yesterday? I so longed for you and you did not come. It seemed as if the day would never end. I thought that perhaps the Indians had killed you; I thought it might be that I should never see you again; and all the world grew dark as night, I felt so terribly alone. Promise me you will never stay away so long again!"

"Never!" exclaimed Cecil, on the impulse of the moment. An instant later he would have given the world to have recalled the word.

"I am so glad!" she cried, clapping her hands in girlish delight; and he could not pain her by an explanation.

"After a while I will tell her how impossible it is for me to come again," he thought. "I cannot tell her now." And he seized upon every word and look of the lovely unconscious girl, with a hunger of heart born of eight years' starvation.

"Now you must come with me to my lodge; you are my guest, and I shall entertain you. I want you to look at my treasures."

183

Cecil went with her, wondering if they would meet Multnomah at her lodge, and if so, what he would say. He felt that he was doing wrong, yet so sweet was it to be in her presence, so much did her beauty fill the mighty craving of his nature, that it was not possible for him to tear himself away.

Some fifteen minutes' walk brought them to Wallulah's lodge. It was a large building, made of bark set upright against a frame-work of poles, and roofed with cedar boards,—in its external appearance like all Willamette lodges. Several Indian girls, neatly dressed and of more than ordinary intelligence, were busied in various employments about the yard. They looked in surprise at the white man and their mistress, but said nothing. The two entered the lodge. Cecil muttered an exclamation of amazement as he crossed the threshold.

The interior was a glow of color, a bower of richness. Silken tapestries draped and concealed the bark walls; the floor of trodden earth was covered with a superbly figured carpet. It was like the hall of some Asiatic palace. Cecil looked at Wallulah, and her eyes sparkled with merriment at his bewildered expression. "I knew you would be astonished," she cried. "Is not this as fair as anything in your own land? No, wait till I show you another room!"

She led the way to an inner apartment, drew back the tapestry that hung over the doorway, and bade him enter.

Never, not even at St. James or at Versailles, had he seen such magnificence. The rich many-hued products of Oriental looms covered the rough walls; the carpet was like a cushion; mirrors sparkling with 184 gems reflected his figure; luxurious divans invited to repose. Everywhere his eye met graceful draperies and artistically blended colors. Silk and gold combined to make up a scene that was like a dream of fable. Cecil's dazzled eyes wandered over all this splendor, then came back to Wallulah's face again.

"I have seen nothing like this in my own land, not even in the King's palace. How came such beautiful things here among the Indians?"

"They were saved from the vessel that was wrecked. They were my mother's, and she had them arranged thus. This was her lodge. It is mine now. I have never entered any other. I have never been inside an Indian wigwam. My mother forbade it, for fear that I might grow like the savage occupants."

Cecil knew now how she had preserved her grace and refinement amid her fierce and squalid surroundings. Again her face changed and the wistful look came back. Her wild delicate nature seemed to change every moment, to break out in a hundred varying impulses.

"I love beautiful things," she said, drawing a fold of tapestry against her cheek. "They seem half human. I love to be among them and feel their influence. These were my mother's, and it seems as if part of her life was in them. Sometimes, after she died, I used to shut my eyes and put my cheek against the soft hangings and try to think it was the touch of her hand; or I would read from her favorite poets and try to think that I heard her repeating them to me again!"

"Read!" exclaimed Cecil; "then you have books?"

"Oh, yes, I will show you all my treasures."

185

She went into another apartment and returned with a velvet case and a richly enchased casket. She opened the case and took out several rolls of parchment.

"Here they are, my dear old friends, that have told me so many beautiful things."

Cecil unrolled them with a scholar's tenderness. Their touch thrilled him; it was touching again some familiar hand parted from years ago. The parchments were covered with strange characters, in a language entirely unknown to him. The initial letters were splendidly illuminated, the margins ornamented with elaborate designs. Cecil gazed on the scrolls, as one who loves music but who is ignorant of its technicalities might look at a sonata of Beethoven or an opera of Wagner, and be moved by its suggested melodies.

"I cannot read it," he said a little sadly.

"Sometime I will teach you," she replied; "and you shall teach me your own language, and we will talk in it instead of this wretched Indian tongue."

"Tell me something about it now," asked Cecil, still gazing at the unknown lines.

"Not now, there is so much else to talk about; but I will to-morrow."

To-morrow! The word pierced him like a knife. For him, a missionary among barbarians, for her, the betrothed of a savage chief, the morrow could bring only parting and woe; the sweet, fleeting present was all they could hope for. For them there could be no to-morrow. Wallulah, however, did not observe his dejection. She had opened the casket, and now placed it between them as they sat together on 186 the divan. One by one, she took out the contents and displayed them. A magnificent necklace of diamonds, another of pearls; rings, brooches, jewelled bracelets, flashed their splendor on him. Totally ignorant of their great value, she showed them only with a true woman's love of beautiful things, showed them as artlessly as if they were but pretty shells or flowers.

"Are they not bright?" she would say, holding them up to catch the light. "How they sparkle!"

One she took up a little reluctantly. It was an opal, a very fine one. She held it out, turning it in the light, so that he might see the splendid jewel glow and pale.

"Is it not lovely?" she said; "like sun-tints on the snow. But my mother said that in her land it is called the stone of misfortune. It is beautiful, but it brings trouble with it."

He saw her fingers tremble nervously as they held it, and she dropped it from them hurriedly into the casket, as if it were some bright poisonous thing she dreaded to touch.

After a while, when Cecil had sufficiently admired the stones, she put them back into the casket and took it and the parchments away. She came back with her flute, and seating herself, looked at him closely.

"You are sad; there are heavy thoughts on your mind. How is that? He who brings me sunshine must not carry a shadow on his own brow. Why are you troubled?"

The trouble was that he realized now, and was compelled to acknowledge to himself, that he loved 187 this gentle, clinging girl, with a passionate love; that he yearned to take her in his arms and shelter her from the terrible savagery before her; and that he felt it could not, must not be.

"It is but little," he replied. "Every heart has its burden, and perhaps I have mine. It is the lot of man."

She looked at him with a vague uneasiness; her susceptible nature responded dimly to the tumultuous emotions that he was trying by force of will to shut up in his own heart.

"Trouble? Oh, do I not know how bitter it is! Tell me, what do your people do when they have trouble? Do they cut off their hair and blacken their faces, as the Indians do, when they lose one they love?"

"No, they would scorn to do anything so degrading. He is counted bravest who makes the least display of grief and yet always cherishes a tender remembrance of the dead."

"So would I. My mother forbade me to cut off my hair or blacken my face when she died, and so I did not, though some of the Indians thought me bad for not doing so. And your people are not afraid to talk of the dead?"

"Most certainly not. Why should we be? We know that they are in a better world, and their memories are dear to us. It is very sweet sometimes to talk of them."

"But the Willamettes never talk of their dead, for fear they may hear their names spoken and come back. Why should they dread their coming back? Ah, if my mother only *would* come back! How I used to long and pray for it!"

188

Cecil began to talk to her about the love and goodness of God. If he could only see her sheltered in the Divine compassion, he could trust her to slip from him into the unknown darkness of her future. She listened earnestly.

"Your words are good," she said in her quaint phraseology; "and if trouble comes to me again I shall remember them. But I am very happy now."

The warmth and thankfulness of her glance sent through him a great thrill of blended joy and pain.

"You forget," he said, forcing himself to be calm, "that you are soon to leave your home and become the wife of Snoqualmie."

Wallulah raised her hand as if to ward off a blow, her features quivering with pain. She tried to reply, but for an instant the words faltered on her lips. He saw it, and a fierce delight leaped up in his heart. "She does not love him, it is I whom she cares for," he thought; and then he thrust the thought down in indignant self-reproach.

"I do not care for Snoqualmie; I once thought I did, but—"

She hesitated, the quick color flushed her face; for the first time she seemed in part, though not altogether, aware of why she had changed.

For an instant Cecil felt as if he must speak; but the consequences rose before him while the words were almost on his lips. If he spoke and won her love, Multnomah would force her into a marriage with Snoqualmie just the same; and if the iron despot were to consent and give her to Cecil, the result would be a bloody war with Snoqualmie.

"I cannot, I must not," thought Cecil. He rose 189 to his feet; his one impulse was to get away, to fight out the battle with himself. Wallulah grew pale.

"You are going?" she said, rising also. "Something in your face tells me you are not coming back," and she looked at him with strained, sad, wistful eyes.

He stood hesitating, torn by conflicting emotions, not knowing what to do.

"If you do not come back, I shall die," she said simply.

As they stood thus, her flute slipped from her relaxed fingers and fell upon the floor. He picked it up and gave it to her, partly through the born instinct of the gentleman, which no familiarity with barbarism can entirely crush out, partly through the tendency in time of intense mental strain to relieve the mind by doing any little thing.

She took it, lifted it to her lips, and, still looking at him, began to play. The melody, strange, untaught, artless as the song of a wood-bird, was infinitely sorrowful and full of longing. Her very life seemed to breathe through the music in fathomless yearning. Cecil understood the plea, and the tears rushed unbidden into his eyes. All his heart went out to her in pitying tenderness and love; and yet he dared not trust himself to speak.

"Promise to come back," said the music, while her dark eyes met his; "promise to come back. You are my one friend, my light, my all; do not leave me to perish in the dark. I shall die without you, I shall die, I shall die!"

Could any man resist the appeal? Could Cecil, of all men, thrilling through all his sensitive and ardent 190 nature to the music, thrilling still more to a mighty and resistless love?

"I will come back," he said, and parted from her; he dared not trust himself to say another word. But the parting was not so abrupt as to prevent his seeing the swift breaking-forth of light upon the melancholy face that was becoming so beautiful to him and so dear.

191

CHAPTER VI.

THE TWILIGHT TALE.

That eve I spoke those words again,
And then she hearkened what I said.

DANTE ROSSETTI.

The next day the Indians had a great hunt. A circle of men on foot and on horseback was drawn around a large tract of forest on the western side of the Willamette River. Gradually, with much shouting, hallooing, and beating of bushes, the circle closed upon the game within it, like the folds of a mighty serpent.

There was a prodigious slaughter, a mad scene of butchery, in which the Indians exulted like fiends. Late in the afternoon they returned to camp, stained with blood and loaded with the spoils of the chase. Snoqualmie distinguished himself by killing a large bear, and its claws, newly severed and bleeding, were added to his already ample necklace of similar trophies.

Cecil remained in the almost deserted camp. He tried in vain to talk with the few chiefs who had not gone out to join in the hunt. Missionary work was utterly impossible that day. Wallulah and the problem of his love filled his thoughts. His mind, aroused and burning, searched and analyzed the question upon every side.

192

Should he tell Multnomah of Snoqualmie's cruelty, representing his unfitness to be the husband of the gentle Wallulah?

To the stern war-chief that very cruelty would be an argument in Snoqualmie's favor. Should he himself become a suitor for her hand? He knew full well that Multnomah would reject him with disdain; or, were he to consent, it would involve the Willamettes in a war with the haughty and vindictive Cayuse. Finally, should he attempt to fly with her to some other land? Impossible. All the tribes of the northwest were held in the iron grip of Multnomah. They could never escape; and even if they could, the good he had done among the Indians, the good he hoped would grow from generation to generation, would be all destroyed if it were told among them that he who claimed to come to them with a message from God had ended by stealing the chief's daughter. And had he a right to love any one?—had he a right to love at all? God had sent him to do a work among the Indians; was it not wicked for him to so much as look either to the right or to the left till that work was done?

Amid this maze of perplexities, his tense, agonized soul sought in vain for some solution, some conclusion. At times he sat in his lodge and brooded over these things till he seemed wrought up almost to madness, till his form trembled with excitement, and the old pain at his heart grew sharp and deadly.

Then again, trying to shake it off, he went out among the few Indians who were left in the camp and attempted to do missionary work; but enthusiasm was lacking, the glow and tenderness was gone from 193 his words, the grand devotion that had inspired him so long failed him at last. He was no longer a saintly apostle to the Indians; he was only a human lover, torn by stormy human doubts and fears.

Even the Indians felt that some intangible change had come over him, and as they listened their hearts no longer responded to his eloquence; they felt somehow that the life was gone from his words. He saw it too, and it gave him a keen pang.

He realized that the energy and concentration of his character was gone, that a girl's beauty had drawn him aside from the mission on which God had sent him.

"I will go and see her. I will, without letting her know that I love her, give her to understand my position and her own. She shall see how impossible it is for us ever to be aught to each other. And I shall urge her to cling to God and walk in the path he has appointed for her, while I go on in mine."

So thinking, he left his lodge that evening and took the path to Wallulah's home.

Some distance from the encampment he met an Indian funeral procession. The young Willamette runner had died that morning, and now they were bearing him to the river, down which a canoe was to waft the body and the mourners to the nearest *mimaluse* island. The corpse was swathed in skins and tied around with thongs; the father bore it on his shoulder, for the dead had been but a slender lad. Behind them came the mother and a few Indian women. As they passed, the father chanted a rude lament.

"Oh, Mox-mox, my son, why did you go away and 194 leave our wigwam empty? You were not weak nor sickly, and your life was young. Why did you go? Oh, Mox-mox, dead, dead, dead!"

Then the women took up the doleful refrain,—

"Oh, Mox-mox, dead, dead, dead!"

Then the old man again,—

"Oh, Mox-mox, the sun was warm and food was plenty, yet you went away; and when we reach out for you, you are not there. Oh Mox-mox, dead, dead, dead!"

Then the women again,—

"Oh, Mox-mox, dead, dead, dead!"

And so it went on, till they were embarked and the canoe bore them from sight and hearing. Down on some *mimaluse* island or rocky point, they would stretch the corpse out in a canoe, with the bow and arrows and fishing spear used in life beside it; then turn over it another canoe like a cover, and so leave the dead to his long sleep.

The sight gave an added bitterness to Cecil's meditations.

"After all," he thought, "life is so short,—a shadow fleeting onward to the night,—and love is so sweet! Why not open my heart to the bliss it brings? The black ending comes so soon! Why not fling all thought of consequences to the winds, and gather into my arms the love that is offered me? why not know its warmth and thrill for one golden moment, even though that moment ends in death?"

The blood rushed wildly through his veins, but he resolutely put down the temptation. No, he would be faithful, he would not allow himself even to think of such a thing.

195

Reluctantly, as before, the sentinels made way for him and he went on through the wood to the trysting-place, for such it had come to be. She was waiting. But there was no longer the glad illumination of face, the glad springing forward to meet him. She advanced shyly, a delicate color in her cheek, a tremulous grace in her manner, that he had not observed before; the consciousness of love had come to her and made her a woman. Never had she seemed so fair to Cecil; yet his resolution did not falter.

"I have come, you see,—come to tell you that I can come no more, and to talk with you about your future."

Her face grew very pale.

"Are you going away?" she asked sorrowfully, "and shall I never see you again?"

"I cannot come back," he replied gently. The sight of her suffering cut him to the heart.

"It has been much to see you," he continued, while she stood before him, looking downward, without reply. "It has been like meeting one of my own people. I shall never forget you."

She raised her head and strove to answer, but the words died on her lips. How he loathed himself, talking so smoothly to her while he hungered to take her in his arms and tell her how he loved her!

Again he spoke.

"I hope you will be happy with Snoqualmie, and—"

She lifted her eyes with a sudden light flashing in their black depths.

"Do you want me to hate him? Never speak his name to me again!"
196

"He is to be your husband; nay, it is the wish of your father, and the great sachems approve it."

"Can the sachems put love in my heart? Can the sachems make my heart receive him as its lord? Ah, this bitter custom of the father giving his daughter to whomsoever he will, as if she were a dog! And your lips sanction it!"

Her eyes were full of tears. Scarcely realizing what he did, he tried to take her hand. The slender fingers shrank from his and were drawn away.

"I do not sanction it, it is a bitter custom; but it is to be, and I only wished to smooth your pathway. I want to say or do something that will help you when I am gone."

"Do you know what it would be for me to be an Indian's wife? To cut the wood, and carry the water, and prepare the food,—that would be sweet to do for one I loved. But to toil amid dirt and filth for a savage whom I could only abhor, to feel myself growing coarse and squalid with my surroundings,—I could not live!"

She shuddered as she spoke, as if the very thought was horrible.

"You hate this degraded Indian life as much as I do, and yet it is the life you would push me into," she continued, in a tone of mournful heart-broken reproach. It stung him keenly.

"It is not the life I would push you into. God knows I would give my life to take one thorn from yours," The mad longing within him rushed into his voice in spite of himself, making it thrill with a passionate tenderness that brought the color back into her pallid cheek. "But I cannot remain," he 197 went on, "I dare not; all that I can do is to say something that may help you in the future."

She looked at him with dilated eyes full of pain and bewilderment.

"I have no future if you go away. Why must you go? What will be left me after you are gone? Think how long I was here alone after my mother died, with no one to understand me, no one to talk to. Then you came, and I was happy. It was like light shining in the darkness; now it goes out and I can never hope again. Why must you go away and leave Wallulah in the dark?"

There was a childlike plaintiveness and simplicity in her tone; and she came close to him, looking up in his face with wistful, pleading eyes, the beautiful face wan and drawn with bewilderment and pain, yet never so beautiful as now.

Cecil felt the unspeakable cruelty of his attitude toward her, and his face grew white as death in an awful struggle between love and duty. But he felt that he must leave her or be disloyal to his God.

"I do not wish to go away. But God has called me to a great work, and I must do it. I dare not turn aside. You cannot know how dear your presence is to me, or how bitter it is for me to part from you. But our parting must be, else the work I have done among the tribes will be scattered to the winds and the curse of God will be on me as a false and fallen prophet."

He spoke with a kind of fierceness, striving blindly to battle down the mad longing within, and his tones had a harshness that he was too agitated to notice. She drew back involuntarily. There came into her 198 face a dignity he had never seen before. She was but a recluse and a girl, but she was of royal lineage by right of both her parents, and his words had roused a spirit worthy the daughter of Multnomah.

"Am I a weight on you? Are you afraid I will bring a curse upon you? Do not fear, I shall no longer ask you to stay. Wallulah shall take herself out of your life."

She gave him a look full of despair, as if seeing all hope go from her forever; then she said simply, "Farewell," and turned away.

But in spite of her dignity there was an anguish written on her sweet pale face that he could not resist. All his strength of resolve, all his conviction of duty, crumbled into dust as she turned away; and he was conscious only that he loved her, that he could not let her go.

How it happened he never knew, but she was clasped in his arms, his kisses were falling on brow and cheek in a passionate outburst that could be kept back no longer. At first, she trembled in his arms and shrank away from him; then she nestled close, as if sheltering herself in the love that was hers at last. After awhile she lifted a face over which a shadow of pain yet lingered.

"But you said I would bring you a curse; you feared—"

He stopped her with a caress.

"Even curses would be sweet if they came through you. Forget what I said, remember only that I love you!"

And she was content.

Around them the twilight darkened into night; the 199 hours came and went unheeded by these two, wrapped in that golden love-dream which for a moment brings Eden back again to this gray old earth, all desolate as it is with centuries of woe and tears.

But while they talked there was on him a vague dread, an indefinable misgiving, a feeling that he was disloyal to his mission, disloyal to her; that their love could have but one ending, and that a dark one.

Still he strove hard to forget everything, to shut out all the world,— drinking to the full the bliss of the present, blinding his eyes to the pain of the future.

But after they parted, when her presence was withdrawn and he was alone, he felt like a man faithless and dishonored; like a prophet who had bartered the salvation of the people to whom he had been sent, in exchange for a woman's kisses, which could bring him only disgrace and death.

As he went back to the camp in the stillness of midnight, he was startled by a distant roar, and saw through the tree-tops flames bursting from the far-off crater of Mount Hood. The volcano was beginning one of its periodical outbursts. But to Cecil's mind, imbued with the gloomy supernaturalism of early New England, and unconsciously to himself, tinged in later years with the superstition of the Indians among whom he had lived so long, that ominous roar, those flames leaping up into the black skies of night, seemed a sign of the wrath of God.

200

CHAPTER VII.

ORATOR AGAINST ORATOR.

The gravity, fixed attention, and decorum of these sons of the forest was calculated to make for them a most favorable impression.— GRAY: *History of Oregon.*

The next day all the Indians were gathered around the council grove. Multnomah presided, and every sachem was in his place.

There was to be a trial of eloquence,—a tourney of orators, to see which tribe had the best. Only one, the most eloquent of each tribe, was to speak; and Multnomah was to decide who was victor. The mother of Wallulah had introduced the custom, and it had become popular among the Indians.

Cecil was in his place among the chiefs, with worn face and abstracted air; Snoqualmie was present, with hawk-like glance and imperious mien; there was Mishlah, with his sullen and brutal features; there, too, wrapped closely in his robe of fur, sat Tohomish, brooding, gloomy,—the wild empire's mightiest master of eloquence, and yet the most repulsive figure of them all.

The Indians were strangely quiet that morning; the hush of a superstitious awe was upon them. The smoking mountains, Hood and Adams as the white man calls them, Au-poo-tah and Au-ka-ken in the Indian tongue, were becoming active of late. The 201 previous night flame had been seen bursting from the top of Mount Hood and thick black smoke still puffed upward from it, and on Mount Adams rested a heavy cloud of volcanic vapors. Were the mountains angry? Aged men told how in the old time there had been a terrible outburst of flame and ashes from Mount Hood; a rain of fire and stones had fallen over all the Willamette valley; the very earth had trembled at the great mountain's wrath.

As the lower animals feel in the air the signs of a coming storm, so these savages felt, by some kindred intuition, that a mysterious convulsion of Nature was at hand. They talked in low tones, they were subdued in manner; any one coming suddenly upon them would have been impressed by the air of uneasiness and apprehension that everywhere prevailed. But the chiefs were stoical, and Multnomah impassive as ever.

Could it have been that the stormy influences at work in Nature lent energy to the orators that day? They were unusually animated, at least for Indians, though a white man would have found them intolerably bombastic. Each speech was a boastful eulogy of the speaker's tribe, and an exaggerated account of the wonderful exploits of its warriors.

This was rather dangerous ground; for all the tribes had been at enmity in days gone by, and some of their most renowned victories had been won over each other. Every one took it in good part, however, except Mishlah. When We-math, chief of the Klamaths, recounting the exploits of his race, told how in ancient times they had lorded it over the Mollalies, Mishlah glared at him as if tempted to leap upon him and strike him down. Fortunately the orator passed 202 on to other things, and the wrath of the Mollalie chief gradually cooled.

Then came Cecil. It was a grand opening. He could speak of his own people, of their ancient savagery and present splendor, and show how the gospel of love and justice had been the cause of their elevation. Then would come the appeal to the Indians to accept this faith as their own and share in its uplifting power. It was a magnificent opportunity, the opportunity of a life-time.

But the mental conflict he had just passed through had rent his mind like a volcanic upheaval. It possessed no longer the intense concentration which had been the source of its strength. Tenderness, benevolence, missionary zeal, were still there, but no longer sovereign. Other passions divided his heart; a hopeless and burning love consumed his being.

He spoke, but the fire was gone from his delivery and the vividness from his imagination. His eloquence was not what it had been; his heart was no longer in his work, and his oration was a failure.

Even the Indians noticed that something was lacking in his oratory, and it no longer moved them as it had done. Cecil realized it, and strove to speak with more energy, but in vain; he could not arouse himself; and it was with a consciousness of failure that he brought his speech to a close and resumed his seat.

To a man of his morbid conscientiousness only one conclusion was possible.

"God sent me to proclaim salvation to these children of darkness," he thought, "and I have turned aside to fill my heart with a woman's love. His wrath is on me. He has taken his spirit from me. I am 203 a thing rejected and accursed, and this people will go down to death because I have failed in my mission."

While he sat absorbed in these bitter, self-accusing thoughts, the speaking went on. Wau-ca-cus the Klickitat made a strong "talk," picturesque in Indian metaphor, full of energy. But the chief that followed surpassed him. Orator caught fire from orator; thoughts not unworthy a civilized audience were struck out by the intensity of the emulation; speakers rose to heights which they had never reached before, which they were destined never to reach again. In listening to and admiring their champions, the tribes forgot the smoking mountains and the feeling of apprehension that had oppressed them. At length Snoqualmie made a speech breathing his own daring spirit in every word. It went immeasurably beyond the others; it was the climax of all the darkly splendid eloquence of the day.

No, not of all. From his place among the chiefs rose a small and emaciated figure; the blanket that had muffled his face was thrown aside, and the tribes looked on the mis-shapen and degraded features of Tohomish the Pine Voice. He stood silent at first, his eyes bent on the ground, like a man in a trance. For a moment the spectators forgot the wonderful eloquence of the man in his ignoble appearance. What could he do against Wau-ca-cus the Klickitat and

Snoqualmie the Cayuse, whose sonorous utterances still rang in their ears, whose majestic presence still filled their minds!

"The Willamettes are beaten at last,—the Willamette speakers can no more be called the best," was the one exultant thought of the allies, and the Willamettes 204 trembled for the fame of their orators. Back in the shadow of the cottonwoods, an old Willamette warrior put an arrow on the string and bent his bow unseen on Tohomish.

"He cannot beat them, and it shall never be said that Tohomish failed," he muttered. At that moment, even as death hung over him, the orator's voice was heard beginning his "talk;" and the warrior's hand fell, the bent bow was relaxed, the arrow dropped from the string. For with the first accents of that soft and lingering voice the tribes were thrilled as with the beginning of music.

The orator's head was still bent down, his manner abstracted; he spoke of the legends and the glories of the Willamette tribe, but spoke of them as if that tribe belonged to the past, as if it had perished from the earth, and he was telling the tale of a great dead race. His tones were melodious but indescribably mournful. When at length he lifted his face, his eyes shone with a misty light, and his brutal features were illuminated with a weird enthusiasm. A shudder went through the vast and motley assembly. No boastful rant was this, but a majestic story of the past, the story of a nation gone forever. It was the death-song of the Willamettes, solemnly rendered by the last and greatest orator of the race.

At length he spoke of Multnomah and of the power of the confederacy in his time, but spoke of it as of old time, seen dimly through the lapse of years. Then, when as it seemed he was about to go on and tell how this power came to fall, he hesitated; the words faltered on his lips; he suddenly broke off, took his seat, and drew his robe again over his face.

"It was the Death-song of the Willamettes."

205

The effect was indescribable. The portentous nature of the whole speech needed only that last touch of mystery. It sent through every heart a wild and awesome thrill, as at the shadow of approaching destiny.

The multitude were silent; the spell of the prophet's lofty and mournful eloquence still lingered over them. Multnomah rose. With him rested the decision as to who was the greatest orator. But the proud old war-chief knew that all felt that Tohomish had far surpassed his competitors, and he was resolved that not his lips but the voice of the tribes should proclaim their choice.

"Multnomah was to decide who has spoken best, but he leaves the decision with you. You have heard them all. Declare who is the greatest, and your word shall be Multnomah's word."

There was an instant's silence; then in a murmur like the rush of the sea came back the voice of the multitude.

"Tohomish! Tohomish! he is greatest!"

"He is greatest," said Multnomah. But Tohomish, sitting there dejectedly, seemed neither to see nor hear.

"To-morrow," said the war-chief, "while the sun is new, the chiefs will meet in council and the great talk shall be ended. And after it ends, Multnomah's daughter will be given to Snoqualmie, and Multnomah will bestow a rich *potlatch* [a giving of gifts] on the people. And then all will be done."

The gathering broke up. Gradually, as the Indians gazed on the smoking mountains, the excitement produced by the oratory they had just heard wore off. 206 Only Tohomish's sombre eloquence, so darkly in unison with the menacing aspect of Nature, yet lingered in every mind. They were frightened and startled, apprehensive of something to come. Legends, superstitious lore of by-gone time connected with the "smoking mountains," were repeated that afternoon wherever little groups of Indians had met together. Through all these gathered tribes ran a dread yet indefinable whisper of apprehension, like the first low rustle of the leaves that foreruns the coming storm.

Over the valley Mount Adams towered, wrapped in dusky cloud; and from Mount Hood streamed intermittent bursts of smoke and gleams of fire that grew plainer as the twilight fell. Louder, as the hush of evening deepened, came the sullen roar from the crater of Mount Hood. Below the crater, the ice-fields that had glistened in unbroken whiteness the previous day were now furrowed with wide black streaks, from which the vapor of melting snow and burning lava ascended in dense wreaths. Men wiser than these ignorant savages would have said that some terrible convulsion was at hand.

Multnomah's announcement in the council was a dreadful blow to Cecil, though he had expected it. His first thought was of a personal appeal to the chief, but one glance at the iron features of the autocrat told him that it would be a hopeless undertaking. No appeal could turn Multnomah from his purpose. For Cecil, such an undertaking might be death; it certainly would be contemptuous refusal, and would call down on Wallulah the terrible wrath before which the bravest sachem quailed.

207

Cecil left the grove with the other chiefs and found his way to his lodge. There he flung himself down on his face upon his couch of furs. The Indian woman, his old nurse, who still clung to him, was absent, and for some time he was alone. After a while the flap that hung over the entrance was lifted, and some one came in with the noiseless tread of the Indian. Cecil, lying in a maze of bitter thought, became aware of the presence of another, and raised his head. The Shoshone renegade stood beside him. His gaze rested compassionately on Cecil's sad, worn face.

"What is it?" he asked. "Your words were slow and heavy to-day. There was a weight on your spirit; what is it? You said that we were friends, so I came to ask if I could help."

"You are good, and like a brother," replied Cecil, gently, "but I cannot tell you my trouble. Yet this much I can tell,"—and he sat upon the couch, his whole frame trembling with excitement. "I have sinned a grievous sin, therefore the Great Spirit took away the words from my lips to-day. My heart has become evil, and God has punished me."

It was a relief to his over-burdened conscience to say those harsh things of himself, yet the relief was bitter. Over the bronzed face of the Indian came an expression of deep pity.

"The white man tears himself with his own claws like a wounded beast, but it does not give him peace. Has he done evil? Then let him remember what he has so often told the Indians: 'Forsake evil, turn from sin, and the Great Spirit will forgive.' Let my white brother do this, and it will be well with him."

208

He gazed at Cecil an instant longer; then, with a forbearance that more civilized men do not always show, he left the lodge without another word.

But what he said had its effect. Through Cecil's veins leaped the impulse of a sudden resolve,—a resolve that was both triumph and agony. He fell on his knees beside the couch.

"Thou hast shown me my duty by the lips of the Indian, and I will perform it. I will tear this forbidden love from my heart. Father, help me. Once before I resolved to do this and failed. Help me that I fail not now. Give me strength. Give me the mastery over the flesh, O

God! Help me to put this temptation from me. Help me to fulfil my mission."

The struggle was long and doubtful, but the victory was won at last. When Cecil arose from his knees, there was the same set and resolute look upon his face that was there the morning he entered the wilderness, leaving friends and home behind him forever,—the look that some martyr of old might have worn, putting from him the clinging arms of wife or child, going forth to the dungeon and the stake.

"It is done," murmured the white lips. "I have put her from me. My mission to the Indians alone fills my heart. But God help her! God help her!"

For the hardest part of it all was that he sacrificed her as well as himself.

"It must be," he thought; "I must give her up. I will go now and tell her; then I will never look upon her face again. But oh! what will become of her?"

And his long fingers were clinched as in acutest pain. But his sensitive nerves, his intense susceptibilities 209 were held in abeyance by a will that, once roused, was strong even unto death.

He went out. It was dark. Away to the east Mount Hood lifted its blazing crater into the heavens like a gigantic torch, and the roar of the eruption came deep and hoarse through the stillness of night. Once, twice it seemed to Cecil that the ground trembled slightly under his feet. The Indians were huddled in groups watching the burning crest of the volcano. As the far-off flickering light fell on their faces, it showed them to be full of abject fear.

"It is like the end of the world," thought Cecil. "Would that it were; then she and I might die together."

He left the camp and took the trail through the wood to the trysting-place; for, late as it was, he knew that she awaited him.

210

CHAPTER VIII.

IN THE DARK.

There is not one upon life's weariest way,
Who is weary as I am weary of all but death.

SWINBURNE.

The grim sentinels by the pathway, who had been so reluctant to let Cecil pass the day before, were still more reluctant this evening. One of them planted himself in the trail directly in front of Cecil, and did not offer to let him go on, but stood sullenly blocking the way. Cecil touched the warrior's arm and bade him stand aside. For an instant it seemed that he would refuse, but his superstitious respect for the white *tomanowos* overcame his obstinacy,—and he stepped unwillingly back.

But as Cecil went on he felt, and felt rightly, that they would not let him pass again,—that the last act, be it what it might, in his love drama, was drawing to a close.

A few moments' walk, and he saw in the dark the little figure awaiting him under the trees. She came slowly forward to meet him. He saw that her face was very pale, her eyes large and full of woe. She gave him her hands; they felt like ice. He bent over her and kissed her with quivering lips.

"Poor child," he said, putting his arms around her slender form and drawing it close in his embrace, 211 "how can I ever tell you what I have to tell you to-night!"

She did not respond to his caress. At length, looking up in a lifeless, stricken way, she spoke in a mechanical voice, a voice that did not sound like her own,—

"I know it already. My father came and told me that to-morrow I must—" She shuddered; her voice broke; then she threw her arms around his neck and clung to him passionately. "But they can never tear me away from you; never, never!"

How could he tell her that he came to put her away from him, that he came to bid her farewell? He clasped her the tighter in his arms. For an instant his mind swept all the chances of flight with her, only to realize their utter hopelessness; then he remembered that even to think of such a thing was treachery to the resolves he had just made. He shook from head to foot with stormy emotion.

She lifted her head from his breast, where it was pillowed.

"Let us get horses or a canoe, and fly to-night to the desert or the sea,—anywhere, anywhere, only to be away from here! Let us take the trail you came on, and find our way to your people."

"Alas," replied Cecil, "how could we escape? Every tribe, far and near, is tributary to your father. The runners would rouse them as soon as we were missed. The swiftest riders would be on our trail; ambuscades would lurk for us in every thicket; we could never escape; and even if we should, a whole continent swarming with wild tribes lies between us and my land."

212

She looked at him in anguish, with dim eyes, and her arms slipped from around his neck.

"Do you no longer love Wallulah? Something tells me that you would not wish to fly with me, even if we could escape. There is something you have not told me."

Clasping her closely to him, he told her how he felt it was the will of God that they must part. God had sent him on a sacred mission, and he dared not turn aside. Either her love or the redemption of the tribes of the Wauna must be given up; and for their sake love must be sacrificed.

"To-day God took away the words from my lips and the spirit from my heart. My soul was lead. I felt like one accursed. Then it came to me that it was because I turned aside from my mission to love you. We must part. Our ways diverge. I must walk my own pathway alone wheresoever it leads me. God commands, and I must obey."

The old rapt look came back, the old set, determined expression which showed that that delicate organization could grow as strong as granite in its power to endure.

Wallulah shrank away from him, and strove to free herself from his embrace.

"Let me go," she said, in a low, stifled tone. "Oh, if I could only die!"

But he held her close, almost crushing the delicate form against his breast. She felt his heart beat deeply and painfully against her own, and in some way it came to her that every throb was agony, that he was in the extremity of mental and physical suffering.

"God help me!" he said; "how can I give you up?"

213

She realized by woman's intuition that his whole soul was wrung with pain, with an agony darker and bitterer than her own; and the exceeding greatness of his suffering gave her strength. A sudden revulsion of feeling affected her. She looked up at him with infinite tenderness.

"I wish I could take all the pain away from you and bear it myself."

"It is God's will; we must submit to it."

"His will!" Her voice was full of rebellion. "Why does he give us such bitter suffering? Doesn't he care? I thought once that God was good, but it is all dark now."

"Hush, you must not think so. After all, it will be only a little while till we meet in heaven, and there no one can take you from me."

"Heaven is so far off. The present is all that I can see, and it is as black as death. Death! it would be sweet to die now with your arms around me; but to *live* year after year with him! How can I go to him, now that I have known you? How can I bear his presence, his touch?"

She shuddered there in Cecil's arms. All her being shrunk in repugnance at the thought of Snoqualmie.

"Thank God for death!" said Cecil, brokenly.

"It is so long to wait," she murmured, "and I am so young and strong."

His kisses fell on cheek and brow. She drew down his head and put her cheek against his and clung to him as if she would never let him go.

It was a strange scene, the mournful parting of the lovers in the gloom of the forest and the night. To 214 the east, through the black net-work of leaves and branches, a dull red glow marked the crater of Mount Hood, and its intermittent roar came to them through the silence. It was a night of mystery and horror,—a fitting night for their tragedy of love and woe. The gloom and terror of their surroundings seemed to throw a supernatural shadow over their farewell.

"The burning mountain is angry to-night," said Wallulah, at last. "Would that it might cover us up with its ashes and stones, as the Indians say it once did two lovers back in the old time."

"Alas, death never comes to those who wish for it. When the grace and sweetness are all fled from our lives, and we would be glad to lie down in the grave and be at rest, then it is that we must go on living. Now I must go. The longer we delay our parting the harder it will be."

"Not yet, not yet!" cried Wallulah. "Think how long I must be alone,—always alone until I die."

"God help us!" said Cecil, setting his teeth. "I will dash my mission to the winds and fly with you. What if God does forsake us, and our souls are lost! I would rather be in the outer darkness with you than in heaven without you."

His resolution had given way at last. But in such cases, is it not always the woman that is strongest?

"No," she said, "you told me that your God would forsake you if you did. It must not be."

She withdrew herself from his arms and stood looking at him. He saw in the moonlight that her pale tear-stained face had upon it a sorrowful resignation, a mournful strength, born of very hopelessness.

"God keep you, Wallulah!" murmured Cecil, brokenly. 215 "If I could only feel that he would shelter and shield you!"

"That may be as it will," replied the sweet, patient lips. "I do not know. I shut my eyes to the future. I only want to take myself away from you, so that your God will not be angry with you. Up there," she said, pointing, "I will meet you sometime and be with you forever. God will not be angry then. Now farewell."

He advanced with outstretched arms. She motioned him back.

"It will make it harder," she said.

For a moment she looked into his eyes, her own dark, dilated, full of love and sadness; for a moment all that was within him thrilled to the passionate, yearning tenderness of her gaze; then she turned and went away without a word.

He could not bear to see her go, and yet he knew it must end thus; he dared not follow her or call her back. But so intense was his desire for her to return, so vehemently did his life cry out after her, that for an instant it seemed to him he *had* called out, "Come back! come back!" The cry rose to his lips; but he set his teeth and held it back. They *must* part; was it not God's will? The old pain at his heart returned, a faintness was on him, and he reeled to the ground.

Could it be that her spirit felt that unuttered cry, and that it brought her back? Be this as it may, while he was recovering from his deadly swoon he dimly felt her presence beside him, and the soft cool touch of her fingers on his brow. Then—or did he imagine it?—her lips, cold as those of the dead, 216 touched his own. But when consciousness entirely returned, he was alone in the forest.

Blind, dizzy, staggering with weakness, he found his way to the camp. Suddenly, as he drew near it he felt the earth sway and move beneath him like a living thing. He caught hold of a tree to escape being thrown to the ground. There came an awful burst of flame from Mount Hood. Burning cinders and scoria lit up the eastern horizon like a fountain of fire. Then down from the great canyon of the Columbia, from the heart of the Cascade Range, broke a mighty thundering sound, as if half a mountain had fallen. Drowning for a moment the roar of the volcano, the deep echo rolled from crag to crag, from hill to hill. A wild chorus of outcries rang from the startled camp,—the fierce, wild cry of many tribes mad with fear yet breathing forth tremulous defiance, the cry of human dread mingling with the last echoes of that mysterious crash.

217

CHAPTER IX.

QUESTIONING THE DEAD.

Then he said: "Cold lips and breast without breath,
Is there no voice, no language of death?"

While Cecil was on his way that evening to seek Wallulah, a canoe
with but a single occupant was dropping down the Columbia toward
one of the many *mimaluse*, or death-islands, that are washed by its
waters.

An Indian is always stealthy, but there was an almost more than
Indian stealthiness about this canoe-man's movements. Noiselessly,
as the twilight deepened into darkness, the canoe glided out of a
secluded cove not far from the camp; noiselessly the paddle dipped
into the water, and the canoe passed like a shadow into the night.

On the rocky *mimaluse* island, some distance below the mouth of
the Willamette, the Indian landed and drew his boat up on the beach.
He looked around for a moment, glanced at the red glow that lit the
far-off crest of Mount Hood, then turned and went up the pathway
to the ancient burial hut.

Who was it that had dared to visit the island of the dead after dark?
The bravest warriors were not capable of such temerity. Old men
told how, away back in the past, some braves had ventured upon the
island 218 after nightfall, and had paid the awful forfeit. They were
struck by unseen hands. Weapons that had lain for years beside the
decaying corpses of forgotten warriors wounded them in the dark.
Fleeing to their canoes in swiftest fear, they found the shadowy
pursuit was swifter still, and were overtaken and struck down, while
the whole island rung with mocking laughter. One only escaped,
plunging all torn and bruised into the river and swimming to the
farther shore. When he looked back, the island was covered with

moving lights, and the shrill echo of fiendish mirth came to him across the water. His companions were never seen again. A little while afterward the dogs barked all night around his lodge, and in the morning he was found lying dead upon his couch, his face ghastly and drawn with fear, as if at some frightful apparition.

"He disturbed the *mimaluse tillicums* [dead people], and they came for him," said the old medicine men, as they looked at him.

Since then, no one had been on the island except in the daytime. Little bands of mourners had brought hither the swathed bodies of their dead, laid them in the burial hut, lifted the wail over them, and left upon the first approach of evening.

Who, then, was this,—the first for generations to set foot on the *mimaluse illahee* after dark?

It could be but one, the only one among all the tribes who would have dared to come, and to come alone,—Multnomah, the war-chief, who knew not what it was to fear the living or the dead.

Startled by the outburst of the great smoking mountains, which always presaged woe to the Willamettes, 219 perplexed by Tohomish's mysterious hints of some impending calamity, weighed down by a dread presentiment, he came that night on a strange and superstitious errand.

On the upper part of the island, above reach of high water, the burial hut loomed dark and still in the moonlight as the chief approached it.

Some of the Willamettes, like the Chinooks, practised canoe burial, but the greater part laid their dead in huts, as did also the Klickitats and the Cascades.

The war-chief entered the hut. The rude boards that covered the roof were broken and decayed. The moonlight shone through many openings, lighting up the interior with a dim and ghostly radiance. There, swathed in crumbling cerements, ghastly in shrunken flesh and protruding bone, lay the dead of the line of Multnomah,—the chiefs of the blood royal who had ruled the Willamettes for many generations. The giant bones of warriors rested beside the more delicate skeletons of their women, or the skeletons, slenderer still, of little children of the ancient race. The warrior's bow lay beside him with rotting string; the child's playthings were still clasped in fleshless fingers; beside the squaw's skull the ear-pendants of *hiagua* shells lay where they had fallen from the crumbling flesh years before.

Near the door, and where the slanting moonbeams fell full upon it, was the last who had been borne to the death hut, the mother of Wallulah. Six years before Multnomah had brought her body,—brought it alone, with no eye to behold his grief; and since then no human tread had disturbed the royal burial-place.

220

He came now and looked down upon the body. It had been tightly swathed, fold upon fold, in some oriental fabric; and the wrappings, stiffened by time still showed what had once been a rare symmetry of form. The face was covered with a linen cloth, yellow now through age and fitting like a mask to the features. The chief knelt down and drew away the face-cloth. The countenance, though shrunken, was almost perfectly preserved. Indeed, so well preserved were many of the corpses the first white settlers found on these *mimaluse* islands as to cause at one time a belief that the Indians had some secret process of embalming their dead. There was no such process, however,—nothing save the antiseptic properties of the ocean breeze which daily fanned the burial islands of the lower Columbia.

Lovely indeed must the mother of Wallulah have been in her life. Withered as her features were, there was a delicate beauty in them still,—in the graceful brow, the regular profile, the exquisitely chiselled chin. Around the shoulders and the small shapely head her hair had grown in rich luxuriant masses.

The chief gazed long on the shrunken yet beautiful face. His iron features grew soft, as none but Wallulah had ever seen them grow. He touched gently the hair of his dead wife, and put it back from her brow with a wistful, caressing tenderness. He had never understood her; she had always been a mystery to him; the harsh savagery of his nature had never been able to enter into or comprehend the refined grace of hers; but he had loved her with all the fierce, tenacious, secretive power of his being, a 221 power that neither time nor death could change. Now he spoke to her, his low tones sounding weird in that house of the dead,—a strange place for words of love.

"My woman,—mine yet, for death itself cannot take from Multnomah that which is his own; my bird that came from the sea and made its nest for a little while in the heart of Multnomah and then flew away and left it empty,—I have been hungry to see you, to touch your hair and look upon your face again. Now I am here, and it is sweet to be with you, but the heart of Multnomah listens to hear you speak."

He still went on stroking her hair softly, reverently. It seemed the only caress of which he was capable, but it had in it a stern and mournful tenderness.

"Speak to me! The dead talk to the *tomanowos* men and the dreamers. You are mine; talk to me; I am in need. The shadow of something terrible to come is over the Willamette. The smoking mountains are angry; the dreamers see only bad signs; there are black things before Multnomah, and he cannot see what they are. Tell me,—the dead are wise and know that which comes,—what is this unknown evil which threatens me and mine?"

He looked down at her with intense craving, intense desire, as if his imperious will could reanimate that silent clay and force to the mute lips the words he so desired. But the still lips moved not, and the face lay cold under his burning and commanding gaze. The chief leaned closer over her; he called her name aloud,—something that the Willamette Indians rarely did, for they believed that if the names of the dead 222 were spoken, even in conversation, it would bring them back; so they alluded to their lost ones only indirectly, and always reluctantly and with fear.

"Come back!" said he, repeating the name he had not spoken for six years. "You are my own, you are my woman. Hear me, speak to me, you whom I love; you who, living or dead, are still the wife of Multnomah."

No expression flitted over the changeless calm of the face beneath him: no sound came back to his straining ears except the low intermittent roar of the far-off volcano.

A sorrowful look crossed his face. As has been said, there was an indefinable something always between them, which perhaps must ever be between those of diverse race. It had been the one mystery that puzzled him while she was living, and it seemed to glide, viewless yet impenetrable, between them now. He rose to his feet.

"It comes between us again," he thought, looking down at her mournfully. "It pushed me back when she was living, and made me feel that I stood outside her heart even while my arms were around her. It comes between us now and will not let her speak. If it was only something I could see and grapple with!"

And the fierce warrior felt his blood kindle within him, that not only death but something still more mysterious and incomprehensible should separate him from the one he loved. He turned sadly away and passed on to the interior of the hut. As he gazed on the crumbling relics of humanity around him, the wonted look of command came back to his brow. These *should* obey; by iron strength of will and mystic 223 charm he would sway them to his bidding. The withered lips of death, or spirit voices, should tell him what he wished to know. Abjectly superstitious as was the idea it involved, there was yet something grand in his savage despotic grasp after power that, dominating all he knew of earth, sought to bend to his will even the spirit-land.

The chief believed that the departed could talk to him if they would; for did they not talk to the medicine men and the dreamers? If so, why not to him, the great chief, the master of all the tribes of the Wauna?

He knelt down, and began to sway his body back and forth after the manner of the Nootka *shamans*, and to chant a long, low, monotonous song, in which the names of the dead who lay there were repeated over and over again.

"Kamyah, Tlesco, Che-aqah, come back! come back and tell me the secret, the black secret, the death secret, the woe that is to come. Winelah, Sic-mish, Tlaquatin, the land is dark with signs and omens; the hearts of men are heavy with dread; the dreamers say that the end is come for Multnomah and his race. Is it true? Come and tell me. I wait, I listen, I speak your names; come back, come back!"

Tohomish himself would not have dared to repeat those names in the charnel hut, lest those whom he invoked should spring upon him and tear him to pieces. No more potent or more perilous charm was known to the Indians.

Ever as Multnomah chanted, the sullen roar of the volcano came like an undertone and filled the pauses of the wild incantation. And as he went on, it 224 seemed to the chief that the air grew thick with ghostly presences. There was a sense of breathing life all around him. He felt that others, many others, were with him; yet he saw nothing. When he paused for some voice, some whisper of reply, this sense of hyper-physical perception became so acute that he could almost *see*, almost *hear*, in the thick blackness and the silence; yet no answer came.

Again he resumed his mystic incantation, putting all the force of his nature into the effort, until it seemed that even those shadowy things of the night must yield to his blended entreaty and command. But there came no response. Thick and thronging the viewless presences seemed to gather, to look, and to listen; but no reply came to his ears, and no sight met his eyes save the swathed corpses and the white-gleaming bones on which the shifting moonbeams fell.

Multnomah rose to his feet, baffled, thwarted, all his soul glowing with anger that he should be so scorned.

"Why is this?" said his stern voice in the silence. "You come, but you give no reply; you look, you listen, but you make no sound. Answer me, you who know the future; tell me this secret!"

Still no response. Yet the air seemed full of dense, magnetic life, of muffled heart-beats, of voiceless, unresponsive, uncommunicative forms that he could almost touch.

For perhaps the first time in his life the war-chief found himself set at naught. His form grew erect; his eyes gleamed with the terrible wrath which the tribes dreaded as they dreaded the wrath of the Great Spirit.

"Come back! Come back!"

225

"Do you mock Multnomah? Am I not war-chief of the Willamettes? Though you dwell in shadow and your bodies are dust, you are Willamettes, and I am still your chief. Give up your secret! If the Great Spirit has sealed your lips so that you cannot speak, give me a sign that will tell me. Answer by word or sign; I say it,—I, Multnomah, your chief and master."

Silence again. The roar of the volcano had ceased; and an ominous stillness brooded over Nature, as if all things held their breath, anticipating some mighty and imminent catastrophe. Multnomah's hands were clinched, and his strong face had on it now a fierceness of command that no eye had ever seen before. His indomitable will reached out to lay hold of those unseen presences and compel them to reply.

A moment of strained, commanding expectation: then the answer came; the sign was given. The earth shook beneath him till he staggered, almost fell; the hut creaked and swayed like a storm-driven wreck; and through the crevices on the side toward Mount Hood came a blinding burst of flame. Down from the great gap in the Cascade Range through which flows the Columbia rolled the far-off thundering crash which had so startled Cecil and appalled the tribes. Then, tenfold louder than before, came again the roar of the volcano.

Too well Multnomah knew what had gone down in that crash; too well did he read the sign that had been given. For a moment it seemed as if all the strength of his heart had broken with that which had fallen; then the proud dignity of his character reasserted itself, even in the face of doom.

226

"It has come at last, as the wise men of old said it would. The end is at hand; the Willamettes pass like a shadow from the earth. The Great Spirit has forsaken us, our *tomanowos* has failed us. But my own heart fails me not, and my own arm is strong. Like a war-chief will I meet that which is to come. Multnomah falls, but he falls as the Bridge has fallen, with a crash that will shake the earth, with a ruin that shall crush all beneath him even as he goes down."

Turning away, his eyes fell on the body of his wife as he passed toward the door. Aroused and desperate as he was, he stopped an instant and looked down at her with a long, lingering look, a look that seemed to say, "I shall meet you ere many suns. Death and ruin but give you back to me the sooner. There will be nothing between us then; I shall understand you at last."

Then he drew his robe close around him, and went out into the night.

BOOK V.

THE SHADOW OF THE END.

CHAPTER I.

THE HAND OF THE GREAT SPIRIT.

"We view as one who hath an evil sight,"
He answered, "plainly objects far remote."

CAREY: *Dante.*

The night came to an end at last,—a night not soon forgotten by the Oregon Indians, and destined to be remembered in tale and *tomanowos* lore long after that generation had passed away. The sky was thick with clouds; the atmosphere was heavy with smoke, which, dense and low-hanging in the still weather, shut out the entire horizon. The volcano was invisible in the smoky air, but its low mutterings came to them from time to time.

The chiefs met early in the grove of council. Multnomah's countenance told nothing of the night before, but almost all the rest showed something yet of superstitious fear. Mishlah's face was haggard, his air startled and uneasy, like that of some forest animal that had been terribly frightened; and even Snoqualmie looked worn. But the greatest change of all was in Tohomish. His face was as ghastly as that 228 of a corpse, and he came into the council walking in a dull lifeless way, as if hardly aware of what he was doing. Those nearest to him shrank away, whispering to one another that the seer looked like a dead man.

Cecil came last. The severe mental conflict of the past night had told almost fatally on a frame already worn out by years of toil and sickness. His cheek was pale, his eye hollow, his step slow and faltering like one whose flame of life is burning very low. The pain at his heart, always worse in times of exhaustion, was sharp and piercing.

He looked agitated and restless; he had tried hard to give Wallulah into the hands of God and feel that she was safe, but he could not.

For himself he had no thought; but his whole soul was wrung with pain for her. By virtue of his own keen sympathies, he anticipated and felt all that the years had in store for her,—the loneliness, the heartache, the trying to care for one she loathed; until he shrank from her desolate and hopeless future as if it had been his own. All his soul went out to her in yearning tenderness, in passionate desire to shield her and to take away her burden.

But his resolution never wavered. Below the ebb and flow of feeling, the decision to make their separation final was as unchanging as granite. He could not bear to look upon her face again; he could not bear to see her wedded to Snoqualmie. He intended to make one last appeal to the Indians this morning to accept the gospel of peace; then he would leave the council before Wallulah was brought to it. So he sat there now, waiting for the "talk" to begin.

229

The bands gathered around the grove were smaller than usual. Many had fled from the valley at dawn to escape from the dreaded vicinity of the smoking mountains; many hundreds remained, but they were awed and frightened. No war could have appalled them as they were appalled by the shaking of the solid earth under their feet. All the abject, superstition of their natures was roused. They looked like men who felt themselves caught in the grasp of some supernatural power.

Multnomah opened the council by saying that two runners had arrived with news that morning; the one from the sea-coast, the other from up the Columbia. They would come before the council and tell the news they had brought.

The runner from the upper Columbia spoke first. He had come thirty miles since dawn. He seemed unnerved and fearful, like one about to announce some unheard-of calamity. The most stoical bent forward eagerly to hear.

"The Great Spirit has shaken the earth, and the Bridge of the Gods has fallen!"

There was the silence of amazement; then through the tribes passed in many tongues the wild and wondering murmur, "The Bridge of the Gods has fallen! The Bridge of the Gods has fallen!" With it, too, went the recollection of the ancient prophecy that when the Bridge fell the power of the Willamettes would also fall. Now the Bridge was broken, and the dominion of the Willamettes was broken forever with it. At another time the slumbering jealousy of the tribes would have burst forth in terrific vengeance on the doomed race. But they were dejected and 230 afraid. In the fall of the Bridge they saw the hand of the Great Spirit, a visitation of God. And so Willamette and tributary alike heard the news with fear and apprehension. Only Multnomah, who knew the message before it was spoken, listened with his wonted composure.

"It is well," he said, with more than Indian duplicity; "the daughter of Multnomah is to become the wife of Snoqualmie the Cayuse, and the new line that commences with their children will give new chiefs to head the confederacy of the Wauna. The old gives way to the new. That is the sign that the Great Spirit gives in the fall of the Bridge. Think you it means that the war-strength is gone from us, that we shall no longer prevail in battle? No, no! who thinks it?"

The proud old sachem rose to his feet; his giant form towered over the multitude, and every eye fell before the haughty and scornful glance that swept council and audience like a challenge to battle.

"Is there a chief here that thinks it? Let him step out, let him grapple with Multnomah in the death-grapple, and see. Is there a tribe that thinks it? We reach out our arms to them; we are ready. Let them meet us in battle now, to-day, and know if our hearts have become the hearts of women. Will you come? We will give you dark and bloody proof that our tomahawks are still sharp and our arms are strong."

He stood with outstretched arms, from which the robe of fur had fallen back. A thrill of dread went through the assembly at the grim defiance; then Snoqualmie spoke.

231

"The heart of all the tribes is as the heart of Multnomah. Let there be peace."

The chief resumed his seat. His force of will had wrung one last victory from fate itself. Instantly, and with consummate address, Multnomah preoccupied the attention of the council before anything could be said or done to impair the effect of his challenge. He bade the other runner, the one from the sea-coast, deliver his message.

It was, in effect, this:—

A large canoe, with great white wings like a bird, had come gliding over the waters to the coast near the mouth of the Wauna. Whence it came no one could tell; but its crew were pale of skin like the great white *shaman* there in the council, and seemed of his race. Some of them came ashore in a small canoe to trade with the Indians, but trouble rose between them and there was a battle. The strangers slew many Indians with their magic, darting fire at them from long black tubes. Then they escaped to the great canoe, which spread its wings and passed away from sight into the sea. Many of the Indians were killed, but none of the pale-faced intruders. Now the band who had suffered demanded that the white man of whom they had heard— the white chief at the council—be put to death to pay the blood-debt.

All eyes turned on Cecil, and he felt that his hour was come. Weak, exhausted in body and mind, wearied almost to death, a sudden and awful peril was on him. For a moment his heart sank, his brain grew dizzy. How *could* he meet this emergency? All his soul went out to God with a dumb prayer for help, with an overwhelming sense of weakness. Then he 232 heard Multnomah speaking to him in cold, hard tones.

"The white man has heard the words of the runner. What has he to say why his life should not pay the blood-debt?"

Cecil rose to his feet. With one last effort he put Wallulah, himself, his mission, into the hands of God; with one last effort he forced himself to speak.

Men of nervous temperament, like Cecil, can bring out of an exhausted body an energy, an outburst of final and intense effort, of which those of stronger physique do not seem capable. But it drains the remaining vital forces, and the reaction is terrible. Was it this flaming-up of the almost burned-out embers of life that animated Cecil now? Or was it the Divine Strength coming to him in answer to prayer? Be this as it may, when he opened his lips to speak, all the power of his consecration came back; physical weakness and mental anxiety left him; he felt that Wallulah was safe in the arms of the Infinite Compassion; he felt his love for the Indians, his deep yearning to help them, to bring them to God, rekindling within him; and never had he been more grandly the Apostle to the Indians than now.

In passionate tenderness, in burning appeal, in living force and power of delivery, it was the supreme effort of his life. He did not plead for himself; he ignored, put aside, forgot his own personal danger; but he set before his hearers the wickedness of their own system of retaliation and revenge; he showed them how it overshadowed their lives and lay like a deadening weight on their better natures. The horror, the cruelty, the brute animalism of the blood-thirst, the 233 war-lust, was set over against the love and forgiveness to which the Great Spirit called them.

The hearts of the Indians were shaken within them. The barbarism which was the outcome of centuries of strife and revenge, the dark and cumulative growth of ages, was stirred to its core by the strong and tender eloquence of this one man. As he spoke, there came to all those swarthy listeners, in dim beauty, a glimpse of a better life; there came to them a moment's fleeting revelation of something above their own vindictiveness and ferocity. That vague longing, that indefinable wistfulness which he had so often seen on the faces of his savage audiences was on nearly every face when he closed.

As he took his seat, the tide of inspiration went from him, and a deadly faintness came over him. It seemed as if in that awful reaction the last spark of vitality was dying out; but somehow, through it all, he felt at peace with God and man. A great quiet was upon him; he was anxious for nothing, he cared for nothing, he simply rested as on the living presence of the Father.

Upon the sweet and lingering spell of his closing words came Multnomah's tones in stern contrast.

"What is the word of the council? Shall the white man live or die?"

Snoqualmie was on his feet in an instant.

"Blood for blood. Let the white man die at the torture-stake."

One by one the chiefs gave their voice for death. Shaken for but a moment, the ancient inherited barbarism which was their very life reasserted itself, and 234 they could decide no other way. One, two, three of the sachems gave no answer, but sat in silence. They were men whose hearts had been touched before by Cecil, and who were already desiring the better life They could not condemn their teacher.

At length it came to Tohomish. He arose. His face, always repulsive, was pallid now in the extreme. The swathed corpses on *mimaluse* island looked not more sunken and ghastly.

He essayed to speak; thrice the words faltered on his lips; and when at last he spoke, it was in a weary, lifeless way. His tones startled the audience like an electric shock. The marvellous power and sweetness were gone from his voice; its accents were discordant, uncertain. Could the death's head before them be that of Tohomish? Could those harsh and broken tones be those of the Pine Voice? He seemed like a man whose animal life still survived, but whose soul was dead.

What he said at first had no relation to the matter before the council. Every Indian had his *tomanowos* appointed him by the Great Spirit from his birth, and that *tomanowos* was the strength of his life. Its influence grew with his growth; the roots of his being were fed in it; it imparted its characteristics to him. But the name and nature of his *tomanowos* was the one secret that must go with him to the grave. If it was told, the charm was lost and the *tomanowos* deserted him.

Tohomish's *tomanowos* was the Bridge and the foreknowledge of its fall: a black secret that had darkened his whole life, and imparted the strange and mournful mystery to his eloquence. Now that the Bridge was 235 fallen, the strength was gone from Tohomish's heart, the music from his words.

"Tohomish has no voice now," he continued; "he is as one dead. He desires to say only this, then his words shall be heard no more among men. The fall of the Bridge is a sign that not only the Willamettes but all the tribes of the Wauna shall fall and pass away. Another people shall take our place, another race shall reign in our stead, and the Indian shall be forgotten, or remembered only as a dim memory of the past.

"And who are they who bring us our doom? Look on the face of the white wanderer there; listen to the story of your brethren slain at the sea-coast by the white men in the canoe, and you will know. They come; they that are stronger, and push us out into the dark. The white wanderer talks of peace; but the Great Spirit has put death between the Indian and the white man, and where he has put death there can be no peace.

"Slay the white man as the white race will slay your children in the time that is to come. Peace? love? There can be only war and hate. Striking back blow for blow like a wounded rattlesnake, shall the red man pass; and when the bones of the last Indian of the Wauna lie bleaching on the prairie far from the *mimaluse* island of his fathers, then there will be peace.

"Tohomish has spoken; his words are ended, and ended forever."

The harsh, disjointed tones ceased. All eyes fell again on Cecil, the representative of the race by which the Willamettes were doomed. The wrath of all those hundreds, the vengeance of all those gathered tribes 236 of the Wauna, the hatred of the whole people he had come to save, seemed to rise up and fall upon him the frail invalid with the sharp pain throbbing at his heart.

But that strange peace was on him still, and his eyes, dilated and brilliant in the extremity of physical pain, met those lowering brows with a look of exceeding pity.

Multnomah rose to pronounce sentence. For him there could be but one decision, and he gave it,—the clinched hand, the downward gesture, that said, "There is death between us. We will slay as we shall be slain."

Cecil was on his feet, though it seemed as if he must fall within the moment. He fought down the pain that pierced his heart like a knife; he gathered the last resources of an exhausted frame for one more effort. The executioners sprang forward with the covering for his eyes that was to shut out the light forever. His glance, his gesture held them back; they paused irresolutely, even in the presence of Multnomah; weak as Cecil was, he was the great white *tomanowos* still, and they dared not touch him. There was a pause, an intense silence.

"I gave up all to come and tell you of God, and you have condemned me to die at the torture-stake," said the soft, low voice, sending through their stern hearts its thrill and pathos for the last time. "But you shall not bring this blood-stain upon your souls. The hand of the Great Spirit is on me; he takes me to himself. Remember—what I have said. The Great Spirit loves you. Pray—forgive—be at peace. Remember—"

237

The quiver of agonizing pain disturbed the gentleness of his look; he reeled, and sank to the ground. For a moment the slight form shuddered convulsively and the hands were clinched; then the struggle ceased and a wonderful brightness shone upon his face. His lips murmured something in his own tongue, something into which came the name of Wallulah and the name of God. Then his eyes grew dim and he lay very still. Only the expression of perfect peace still rested on the face. Sachems and warriors gazed in awe upon the beauty, grand in death, of the one whom the Great Spirit had taken from them. Perhaps the iron heart of the war-chief was the only one that did not feel remorse and self-reproach.

Ere the silence was broken, an old Indian woman came forward from the crowd into the circle of chiefs. She looked neither to the right nor to the left, but advanced among the warrior-sachems, into whose presence no woman had dared intrude herself, and bent over the dead. She lifted the wasted body in her arms and bore it away, with shut lips and downcast eyes, asking no permission, saying no word. The charm that had been around the white *shaman* in life seemed to invest her with its power; for grim chieftains made way, the crowd opened to let her pass, and even Multnomah looked on in silence.

That afternoon, a little band of Indians were assembled in Cecil's lodge. Some of them were already converts; some were only awakened and impressed; but all were men who loved him.

They were gathered, men of huge frame, around a dead body that lay upon a cougar skin. Their faces were sad, their manner was solemn. In the corner 238 sat an aged squaw, her face resting in her hands, her long gray hair falling dishevelled about her shoulders. In that heart-broken attitude she had sat ever since bringing Cecil to the hut. She did not weep or sob but sat motionless, in stoical, dumb despair.

Around the dead the Indians stood or sat in silence, each waiting for the other to say what was in the hearts of all. At length the Shoshone renegade who had so loved Cecil, spoke.

"Our white brother is gone from us, but the Great Spirit lives and dies not. Let us turn from blood and sin and walk in the way our brother showed us. He said, 'Remember;' and shall we forget? I choose now, while he can hear me, before he is laid in the cold ground. I put away from me the old heart of hate and revenge. I ask the Great Spirit to give me the new heart of love and peace. I have chosen."

One by one each told his resolve, the swarthy faces lighting up, the stern lips saying unwonted words of love. Dim and misty, the dawn had come to them; reaching out in the dark, they had got hold of the hand of God and felt that he was a Father. One would have said that their dead teacher lying there heard their vows, so calm and full of peace was the white still face.

That night the first beams of the rising moon fell on a new-made grave under the cottonwoods, not far from the bank of the river. Beneath it, silent in the last sleep, lay the student whose graceful presence had been the pride of far-off Magdalen, the pastor whose memory still lingered in New England, the evangelist whose burning words had thrilled the tribes of the wilderness like the words of some prophet of old.

239

Beside the grave crouched the old Indian woman, alone and forsaken in her despair,—the one mourner out of all for whom his life had been given.

No, not the only one; for a tall warrior enters the grove; the Shoshone renegade bends over her and touches her gently on the shoulder.

"Come," he says kindly, "our horses are saddled; we take the trail up the Wauna to-night, I and my friends. We will fly from this fated valley ere the wrath of the Great Spirit falls upon it. Beyond the mountains I will seek a new home with the Spokanes or the Okanogans. Come; my home shall be your home, because you cared for him that is gone."

She shook her head and pointed to the grave.

"My heart is there; my life is buried with him. I cannot go."

Again he urged her.

"No, no," she replied, with Indian stubbornness; "I cannot leave him. Was I not like his mother? How can I go and leave him for others? The roots of the old tree grow not in new soil. If it is pulled up it dies."

"Come with me," said the savage, with a gentleness born of his new faith. "Be *my* mother. We will talk of him; you shall tell me of him and his God. Come, the horses wait."

Again she shook her head; then fell forward on the grave, her arms thrown out, as if to clasp it in her embrace. He tried to lift her; her head fell back, and she lay relaxed and motionless in his arms.

Another grave was made by Cecil's; and the little band rode through the mountain pass that night, toward the country of the Okanogans, without her.

240

And that same night, an English exploring vessel far out at sea sailed southward, leaving behind the unknown shores of Oregon,—her crew never dreaming how near they had been to finding the lost wanderer, Cecil Grey.

241

CHAPTER II.

THE MARRIAGE AND THE BREAKING UP.

Remembering love and all the dead delight,
And all that time was sweet with for a space.

SWINBURNE.

After Cecil had been borne from the council-grove, the Indians, rousing themselves from the spell of the strange scene they had just witnessed, looked around for Tohomish the seer. He was gone. No one could remember seeing him go, yet he was missing from his accustomed place, and never was he seen or heard of more. Upon his fate, lost in the common ruin that engulfed his race, the legend casts no ray of light. It is certain that the fall of the Bridge, with which his life was interwoven, had a disastrous effect upon him, and as he said, that the strength of his life was broken. It is probable that the orator-seer, feeling within himself that his power was gone, crept away into the forest to die. Perhaps, had they searched for him, they would have found him lying lifeless upon the leaves in some dense thicket or at the foot of some lonely crag.

Whatever his fate, the Indians never looked upon his face again.

Multnomah made no comment on the death of Cecil, or on the prophecy of Tohomish, so much at variance with his own interpretation of the fall of the 242 Bridge. Whatever he had to say was evidently held in reserve for the closing talk with which he would soon dismiss the council.

"You shall see Multnomah's daughter given to Snoqualmie, and then Multnomah will open his hand and make you rich."

So said the war-chief; and a runner was dispatched with a summons to Wallulah. In a little while a band of Indian girls was seen approaching the grove. Surrounded by the maidens, as if they were a guard of honor, came Wallulah, all unconscious of the tragedy that had just been enacted.

Among the chiefs they passed, and stopped before Multnomah. As they paused, Wallulah looked around for Cecil in one quick glance; then, not seeing him, she cast down her eyes despondingly. Multnomah rose and beckoned Snoqualmie to him. He came forward and stood beside the war-chief. The Indian girls stepped back a little, in involuntary awe of the two great sachems, and left Wallulah standing alone before them.

Her face wore a patient look, as of one who is very worn and weary, tired of the burdens of life, yet going forward without hope, without thought even, to other and still heavier burdens. She was clad in a soft oriental fabric; her hair fell in luxuriant tresses upon her shoulders; her flute hung at her belt by a slender chain of gold.

There was something unspeakably sad and heart-broken in her appearance, as she stood there, a listless, dejected figure, before those two grim warriors, awaiting her doom.

Multnomah took her hand; the fingers of the other 243 were clasped around her beloved flute, pressing it closely, as if seeking help from its mute companionship. The chief gave her hand into Snoqualmie's; a shudder passed through her as she felt his touch, and she trembled from head to foot; then she controlled herself by a strong effort. Snoqualmie's fierce black eyes searched her face, as if looking through and through her, and she flushed faintly under their penetrating gaze.

"She is yours," said the war-chief. "Be kind to her, for though she is your wife she is the daughter of Multnomah." So much did the Indian say for love of his child, wondering at her strange, sad look, and feeling vaguely that she was unhappy. She tried to withdraw her fingers from Snoqualmie's clasp the moment her father was done speaking. He held them tightly, however, and bending over her, spoke in a low tone.

"My band starts for home at mid-day. Be ready to go when I send for you."

She looked up with startled, piteous eyes.

"To-day?" she asked in a choked voice.

"To-day," came the abrupt reply; too low for the others to hear, yet harsh enough to sting her through and through. "Do you think Snoqualmie goes back to his *illahee* and leaves his woman behind?"

Her spirit kindled in resentment. Never had the chief's daughter been spoken to so harshly; then all at once it came to her that he *knew*,—that he must have followed Cecil and witnessed one of their last interviews. Jealous, revengeful, the Indian was her master now. She grew pale to the lips. He released her hand, and she shrank away from him, and left the 244 council with her maidens. No one had heard the few half-whispered words that passed between them but those who stood nearest noticed the deadly pallor that came over her face while Snoqualmie was speaking. Multnomah saw it, and Snoqualmie caught from him a glance that chilled even his haughty nature—a glance that said, "Beware; she is the war-chief's daughter."

But even if he had known all, Multnomah would have sacrificed her. His plans must be carried out even though her heart be crushed.

Now followed the *potlatch*,—the giving of gifts. At a signal from the war-chief, his slaves appeared, laden with presents. Large heaps of rich furs and skins were laid on the ground near the chiefs. The finest of bows and arrows, with gaily decorated quivers and store of bow-strings, were brought. Untold treasure of *hiagua* shells, money as well as ornament to the Oregon Indians, was poured out upon the ground, and lay glistening in the sun in bright-colored masses. To the Indians they represented vast and splendid wealth. Multnomah was the richest of all the Indians of the Wauna; and the gifts displayed were the spoil of many wars, treasures garnered during forty years of sovereignty.

And now they were all given away. The chief kept back nothing, except some cases of oriental fabrics that had been saved from the wreck when Wallulah's mother was cast upon the shore. Well would it have been for him and his race had they been given too; for, little as they dreamed it, the fate of the Willamettes lay sealed up in those unopened cases of silk and damask.

245

Again and again the slaves of Multnomah added their burdens to the heaps, and went back for more, till a murmur of wonder rose among the crowd. His riches seemed exhaustless. At length, however, all was brought. The chief stood up, and, opening his hands to them in the Indian gesture for giving, said,—

"There is all that was Multnomah's; it is yours; your hands are full now and mine are empty."

The chiefs and warriors rose up gravely and went among the heaps of treasure; each selecting from furs and skins, arms and *hiagua* shells, that which he desired. There was no unseemly haste or snatching; a quiet decorum prevailed among them. The women and children were excluded from sharing in these gifts, but provisions— dried meats and berries, and bread of *camas* or Wappatto root— were thrown among them on the outskirts of the crowd where they were gathered. And unlike the men, they scrambled for it like hungry animals; save where here and there the wife or daughter of a chief stood looking disdainfully on the food and those who snatched at it.

Such giving of gifts, or *potlatches*, are still known among the Indians. On Puget Sound and the Okanogan, one occasionally hears of some rich Indian making a great *potlatch*,—giving away all his possessions, and gaining nothing but a reputation for disdain of wealth, a reputation which only Indian stoicism would crave. Multnomah's object was not that so much as to make, before the dispersal of the tribes, a last and most favorable impression.

When the presents were all divided, the chiefs resumed their places to hear the last speech of Multnomah,—the speech that closed the council.

246

It was a masterpiece of dignity, subtility, and command. The prophecy of Tohomish was evaded, the fall of the Bridge wrested into an omen propitious to the Willamettes; and at last his hearers found themselves believing as he wished them to believe, without knowing how or why, so strongly did the overmastering personality of Multnomah penetrate and sway their lesser natures. He particularly dwelt on the idea that they were all knit together now and were as one race. Yet through the smooth words ran a latent threat, a covert warning of the result of any revolt against his authority based on what plotting dreamers might say of the fall of the Bridge,—a half-expressed menace, like the gleam of a sword half drawn from the scabbard. And he closed by announcing that ere another spring the young men of all the tribes would go on the warpath against the Shoshones and come back loaded with spoil. And so, kindling the hatred of the chiefs against the common enemy, Multnomah closed the great council.

In a little while the camp was all astir with preparation for departure. Lodges were being taken down, the mats that covered them rolled up and packed on the backs of horses; all was bustle and tumult. Troop after troop crossed the river and took the trail toward the upper Columbia.

But when the bands passed from under the personal influence of Multnomah, they talked of the ominous things that had just happened; they said to each other that the Great Spirit had forsaken the Willamettes, and that when they came into the valley again it would be to plunder and to slay. Multnomah had stayed the tide but for a moment. The fall of 247 the ancient *tomanowos* of the Willamettes had a tremendous significance to the restless tributaries, and already the confederacy of the Wauna was crumbling like a rope of sand. Those tribes would meet no more in peace on the island of council.

248

CHAPTER III.

AT THE CASCADES.

Wails on the wind, fades out the sunset quite,
And in my heart and on the earth is night.

PHILIP BOURKE MARSTON.

The main body of Snoqualmie's followers crossed to the north bank of the Columbia and took the trail leading up the river toward the inland prairies. But Snoqualmie and Wallulah went by canoe as far as the now ruined Bridge of the Gods. There were three canoes in their train. Snoqualmie and Wallulah occupied the first; the other two were laden with the rich things that had once made her lodge so beautiful. It stood all bare and deserted now, the splendor stripped from its rough bark walls even as love and hope had been reft from the heart of its mistress. Tapestries, divans, carpets, mirrors, were heaped in the canoes like spoil torn from the enemy.

The farewell between Wallulah and her father had been sorrowful. It was remembered afterward, by those who were witnesses of it, that the war-chief had shown a tenderness unusual with him, that he had seemed reluctant to part with his daughter, and that she had clung to him, pale and tearful, as if he were her last hope on earth.

When Snoqualmie took her hand to lead her away, she shuddered, withdrew her fingers from his clasp, 249 and walked alone to the canoe. He entered after her: the canoe-men dipped their paddles into the water, and the vessel glided away from the island.

She sat reclining on a heap of furs, her elbows sunk in them, her cheek resting on her hand, her eyes turned back toward her island home. Between it and her the expanse of waters grew ever broader, and the trail the canoe left behind it sparkled in a thousand silvery ripples. The island, with its green prairies and its stately woods, receded fast. She felt as she looked back as if everything was slipping away from her. Lonely as her life had been before Cecil came into it, she had still had her music and her beautiful rooms in the bark lodge; and they seemed infinitely sweet and precious now as she recalled them. Oh, if she could only have them back again! And those interviews with Cecil. How love and grief shook the little figure as she thought! How loathingly she shrunk from the presence of the barbarian at her side! And all the time the island receded farther and farther in the distance, and the canoe glided forward like a merciless fate bearing her on and on toward the savagery of the inland desert.

Snoqualmie sat watching her with glittering, triumphant eyes. To him she was no more than some lovely animal of which he had become the owner; and ownership of course brought with it the right to tantalize and to torture. A malicious smile crossed his lips as he saw how sorrowfully her gaze rested on her old home.

"Look forward," he said, "not back; look forward to your life with Snoqualmie and to the lodge that awaits you in the land of the Cayuses."

250

She started, and her face flushed painfully; then without looking at him she replied,—

"Wallulah loves her home, and leaving it saddens her."

A sparkle of vindictive delight came into his eyes.

"Do the women of the Willamette feel sad when they go to live with their husbands? It is not so with the Cayuse women. They are glad; *they* care for the one they belong to. They love to sit in the sun at the door of the wigwam and say to the other women, 'My man is brave; he leads the war party; he has many scalps at his belt. Who is brave like my man?'"

Wallulah shuddered. He saw it, and the sparkle of malice in his eyes flashed into sudden anger.

"Does the young squaw tremble at these things? Then she must get used to them. She must learn to bring wood and water for Snoqualmie's lodge, too. She must learn to wait on him as an Indian's wife ought. The old wrinkled squaws, who are good for nothing but to be beasts of burden, shall teach her."

There came before her a picture of the ancient withered hags, the burden-bearers, the human vampires of the Indian camps, the vile in word and deed, the first to cry for the blood of captives, the most eager to give taunts and blows to the helpless; were they to be her associates, her teachers? Involuntarily she lifted her hand, as if to push from her a future so dreadful.

"Wallulah will bring the wood and the water. Wallulah will work. The old women need not teach her."

"That is well. But one thing more you must 251 learn; and that is to hold up your head and not look like a drooping captive. Smile, laugh, be gay. Snoqualmie will have no clouded face, no bent head in his lodge."

She looked at him imploringly. The huge form, the swarthy face, seemed to dominate her, to crush her down with their barbarian strength and ferocity. She dropped her eyes again, and lay there on the furs like some frightened bird shrinking from the glance of a hawk.

"I will work; I will bear burdens," she repeated, in a trembling tone. "But I cannot smile and laugh when my heart is heavy."

He watched her with a half angry, half malicious regard, a regard that seemed ruthlessly probing into every secret of her nature.

She knew somehow that he was aware of her love for Cecil, and she dreaded lest he should taunt her with it. Anything but that. He knew it, and held it back as his last and most cruel blow. Over his bronzed face flitted no expression of pity. She was to him like some delicate wounded creature of the forest, that it was a pleasure to torture. So he had often treated a maimed bird or fawn,—tantalizing it, delighted by its fluttering and its pain, till the lust of torture was gratified and the death-blow was given.

He sat regarding her with a sneering, malicious look for a little while; then he said,—

"It is hard to smile on Snoqualmie; but the white man whom you met in the wood, it was not so with him. It was easy to smile and look glad at him, but it is hard to do so for Snoqualmie."

252

Wallulah shrunk as if he had struck her a blow; then she looked at him desperately, pleadingly.

"Do not say such cruel things. I will be a faithful wife to you. I will never see the white man again."

The sneering malice in his eyes gave way to the gleam of exultant anger.

"Faithful! You knew you were to be my woman when you let him put his arms around you and say soft things to you. Faithful! You would leave Snoqualmie for him now, could it be so. But you say well that you will never see him again."

She gazed at him in terror.

"What do you mean? Has anything happened to him? Have they harmed him?"

Over the chief's face came the murderous expression that was there when he slew the Bannock warrior at the torture stake.

"Harmed him! Do you think that he could meet you alone and say sweet things to you and caress you,—you who were the same as my squaw,—and I not harm him? He is dead; I slew him."

False though it was, in so far as Snoqualmie claimed to have himself slain Cecil, it was thoroughly in keeping with Indian character. White captives were often told, "I killed your brother," or, "This is your husband's scalp," when perhaps the person spoken of was alive and well.

"Dead!"

He threw his tomahawk at her feet.

"His blood is on it. You are Snoqualmie's squaw; wash it off."

Dead, dead, her lover was dead! That was all she 253 could grasp. Snoqualmie's insulting command passed unheeded. She sat looking at the Indian with bright, dazed eyes that saw nothing. All the world seemed blotted out.

"I tell you that he is dead, and I slew him. Are you asleep that you stare at me so? Awaken and do as I bid you; wash your lover's blood off my tomahawk."

At first she had been stunned by the terrible shock, and she could realize only that Cecil was dead. Now it came to her, dimly at first, then like a flash of fire, that Snoqualmie had slain him. All her spirit leaped up in uncontrollable hatred. For once, she was the war-chief's daughter. She drew her skirts away from the tomahawk in unutterable horror; her eyes blazed into Snoqualmie's a defiance and scorn before which his own sunk for the instant.

"You killed him! I hate you. I will never be your wife. You have thrown the tomahawk between us; it shall be between us forever. Murderer! You have killed the one I love. Yes, I loved him; and I hate you and will hate you till I die."

The passion in her voice thrilled even the canoe-men, and their paddle strokes fell confusedly for an instant, though they did not understand; for both Wallulah and Snoqualmie had spoken in the royal tongue of the Willamettes. He sat abashed for an instant, taken utterly by surprise.

Then the wild impulse of defiance passed, and the awful sense of bereavement came back like the falling of darkness over a sinking flame. Cecil was gone from her, gone for all time. The world seemed unreal, empty. She sunk among the furs like one 254 stricken down. Snoqualmie, recovering from his momentary rebuff, heaped bitter epithets and scornful words upon her; but she neither saw nor heard, and lay with wide, bright, staring eyes. Her seeming indifference maddened him still more, and he hurled at her the fiercest abuse. She looked at him vaguely. He saw that she did not even know what he was saying, and relapsed into sullen silence. She lay mute and still, with a strained expression of pain in her eyes. The canoe sped swiftly on.

One desolating thought repeated itself again and again,—the thought of hopeless and irreparable loss. By it past and present were blotted out. By and by, when she awoke from the stupor of despair and realized her future, destined to be passed with the murderer of her lover, what then? But now she was stunned with the shock of a grief that was mercy compared with the awakening that must come.

They were in the heart of the Cascade Mountains, and a low deep roar began to reach their ears, rousing and startling all but Wallulah. It was the sound of the cascades, of the new cataract formed by the fall of the Great Bridge. Rounding a bend in the river they came in sight of it. The mighty arch, the long low mountain of stone, had fallen in, damming up the waters of the Columbia, which were pouring over the sunken mass in an ever-increasing volume. Above, the river, raised by the enormous dam, had spread out like a lake, almost submerging the trees that still stood along the former bank. Below the new falls the river was comparatively shallow, its rocky bed half exposed by the sudden stoppage of the waters.

The Indians gazed with superstitious awe on the 255 vast barrier over which the white and foaming waters were pouring. The unwonted roar of the falls, a roar that seemed to increase every moment as the swelling waters rushed over the rocks; the sight of the wreck of the mysterious bridge, foreshadowing the direst calamities,—all this awed the wild children of the desert. They approached the falls slowly and cautiously.

A brief command from Snoqualmie, and they landed on the northern side of the river, not far from the foot of the falls. There they must disembark, and the canoes be carried around the falls on the shoulders of Indians and launched above.

The roar of the Cascades roused Wallulah from her stupor. She stepped ashore and looked in dazed wonder on the strange new world around her. Snoqualmie told her briefly that she must walk up the bank to the place where the canoe was to be launched again above the falls. She listened mutely, and started to go. But the way was steep and rocky; the bank was strewn with the débris of the ruined bridge; and she was unused to such exertion. Snoqualmie saw her stumble and almost fall. It moved him to a sudden and unwonted pity, and he sprang forward to help her. She pushed his hand from her as if it had been the touch of a serpent, and went on alone. His eyes flashed: for all this the reckoning should come, and soon; woe unto her when it came.

The rough rocks bruised her delicately shod feet, the steep ascent took away her breath. Again and again she felt as if she must fall; but the bitter scorn and loathing that Snoqualmie's touch had kindled gave her strength, and at last she completed the ascent.

256

Above the falls and close to them, she sat down upon a rock; a slight, drooping figure, whose dejected pose told of a broken heart.

Before her, almost at her feet, the pent-up river was widened to a vast flood. Here and there a half-submerged pine lifted its crown above it; the surface was ruffled by the wind, and white-crested waves were rolling among the green tree-tops. She looked with indifference upon the scene. She had not heard that the Bridge had fallen, and was, of course, ignorant of these new cascades; and they did not impress her as being strange.

Her whole life was broken up; all the world appeared shattered by the blow that had fallen on her, and nothing could startle her now. She felt dimly that some stupendous catastrophe had taken place; yet it did not appear unnatural. A strange sense of unreality possessed her; everything seemed an illusion, as if she were a shadow in a land of shadows. The thought came to her that she was dead, and that her spirit was passing over the dim ghost trail to the shadow-land. She tried to shake off the fancy, but all was so vague and dreamlike that she hardly knew where or what she was; yet over it all brooded the consciousness of dull, heavy, torturing pain, like the dumb agony that comes to us in fevered sleep, burdening our dreams with a black oppressing weight of horror.

Her hand, hanging listlessly at her side, touched her flute, which was still suspended from her belt by the golden chain. She raised it to her lips, but only a faint inharmonious note came from it. The music seemed gone from the flute, as hope was gone from 257 her heart. To her overwrought nerves, it was the last omen of all. The flute dropped from her fingers; she covered her face with her hands, and the hot tears coursed slowly down her cheeks.

Some one spoke to her, not ungently, and she looked up. One of the canoe-men stood beside her. He pointed to the canoe, now launched near by. Snoqualmie was still below, at the foot of the falls, superintending the removal of the other.

Slowly and wearily she entered the waiting canoe and resumed her seat. The Indian paddlers took their places. They told her that the chief Snoqualmie had bidden them take her on without him. He would follow in the other canoe. It was a relief to be free from his presence, if only for a little while; and the sadness on her face lightened for a moment when they told her.

A few quick paddle-strokes, and the boat shot out into the current above the cascades and then glided forward. No, *not* forward. The canoe-men, unfamiliar with the new cataract, had launched their vessel too close to the falls; and the mighty current was drawing it back. A cry of horror burst from their lips as they realized their danger, and their paddles were dashed into the water with frenzied violence. The canoe hung quivering through all its slender length between the desperate strokes that impelled it forward and the tremendous suction that drew it down. Had they been closer to the bank, they might have saved themselves; but they were too far out in the current. They felt the canoe slipping back in spite of their frantic efforts, slowly at first, then more swiftly; and they knew there was no hope.

258

The paddles fell from their hands. One boatman leaped from the canoe with the desperate idea of swimming ashore, but the current instantly swept him under and out of sight; the other sat motionless in his place, awaiting the end with Indian stolidity.

The canoe was swept like a leaf to the verge of the fall and downward into a gulf of mist and spray. As it trembled on the edge of the cataract, and its horrors opened beneath her, Wallulah realized her doom for the first time; and in the moment she realised it, it was upon her. There was a quick terror, a dreamlike glimpse of white plunging waters, a deafening roar, a sudden terrible shock as the canoe was splintered on the rocks at the foot of the fall; then all things were swallowed up in blackness, a blackness that was death.

Below the falls, strong swimmers, leaping into the water, brought the dead to land. Beneath a pine-tree that grew close by the great Columbia trail and not far from the falls, the bodies were laid. The daughter of Multnomah lay in rude state upon a fawn-skin; while at her feet were extended the brawny forms of the two canoe-men who had died with her, and who, according to Indian mythology, were to be her slaves in the Land of the Hereafter. Her face was very lovely, but its mournfulness remained. Her flute, broken in the shock that had killed her, was still attached to her belt. The Indians had placed her hand at her side, resting upon the flute; and they noticed in superstitious wonder that the cold fingers seemed to half close around it, as if they would clasp it lovingly, even in death. Indian women knelt beside her, fanning her face with fragrant 259 boughs of pine. Troop after troop, returning over the trail to their homes, stopped to hear the tale, and to gaze at the dead face that was so wonderfully beautiful yet so sad.

All day long the bands gathered; each stopping, none passing indifferently by. At length, when evening came and the shadow of the wood fell long and cool, the burials began. A shallow grave was scooped at Wallulah's feet for the bodies of the two canoe-men. Then chiefs—for they only might bury Multnomah's daughter—

entombed her in a cairn; being Upper Columbia Indians, they buried her, after the manner of their people, under a heap of stone. Rocks and bowlders were built around and over her body, yet without touching it, until the sad dead face was shut out from view. And still the stones were piled above her; higher and higher rose the great rock-heap, till a mighty cairn marked the last resting-place of Wallulah. And all the time the women lifted the death-wail, and Snoqualmie stood looking on with folded arms and sullen baffled brow. At length the work was done. The wail ceased; the gathering broke up, and the sachems and their bands rode away, Snoqualmie and his troop departing with them.

Only the roar of the cascades broke the silence, as night fell on the wild forest and the lonely river. The pine-tree beside the trail swayed its branches in the wind with a low soft murmur, as if lulling the sorrow-worn sleeper beneath it into still deeper repose. And she lay very still in the great cairn,—the sweet and beautiful dead,—with the grim warriors stretched at her feet, stern guardians of a slumber never to be broken.

260

CHAPTER IV.

MULTNOMAH'S DEATH-CANOE.

Gazing   alone
To him are wild shadows shown.
Deep under deep unknown.

    DANTE ROSSETTI.

If Multnomah was grieved at his daughter's death, if his heart sunk at the unforeseen and terrible blow that left his empire without an heir and withered all his hopes, no one knew it; no eye beheld his woe. Silent he had ever been, and he was silent to the last. The grand, strong face only grew grander, stronger, as the shadows darkened around him; the unconquerable will only grew the fiercer and the more unflinching. But ere the moon that shone first on Wallulah's new-made cairn had rounded to the full, there was that upon him before which even his will bowed and gave way,—death, swift and mysterious. And it came in this wise.

We have told how at the great *potlatch* he gave away his all, even to the bear-skins from his couch, reserving only those cases of Asiatic textures never yet opened,—all that now remained of the richly laden ship of the Orient wrecked long ago upon his coast. They were opened now. His bed was covered with the magnificent fabrics; they were thrown carelessly over the rude walls and seats, half-trailing on the 261 floor; exquisite folds of velvet and damask swept the leaves and dust,—so that all men might see how rich the chief still was, though he had given away so much. And with his ostentation was mixed a secret pride and tenderness that his dead wife had indirectly given him this wealth. The war-chief's woman had brought him these treasures out of the sea; and now that he had given away his all, even to the bare poles of his lodge, she filled it with fine things and made him rich again,—she who had been sleeping for years in the death-hut on *mimaluse* island. Those treasures, ere the vessel that carried them was wrecked, had been sent as a present from one oriental prince to another. Could it be that they had been purposely impregnated with disease, so that while the prince that sent them seemed to bestow a graceful gift, he was in reality taking a treacherous and terrible revenge? Such things were not infrequent in Asiatic history; and even the history of Europe, in the middle ages, tells us of poisoned masks, of gloves and scarfs charged with disease.

Certain it is that shortly after the cases were opened, a strange and fatal disease broke out among Multnomah's attendants. The howling of medicine-men rang all day long in the royal lodge; each day saw swathed corpses borne out to the funeral pyre or *mimaluse* island. And no concoction of herbs,—however skilfully compounded with stone mortar and pestle,—no incantation of medicine-men or steaming atmosphere of sweat-house, could stay the mortality.

At length Multnomah caught the disease. It seemed strange to the Indians that the war-chief should sicken, 262 that Multnomah should show any of the weaknesses of common flesh and blood; yet so it was. But while the body yielded to the inroad of disease, the spirit that for almost half a century had bent beneath it the tribes of the Wauna never faltered. He lay for days upon his couch, his system wasting with the plague, his veins burning with fever, holding death off only by might of will. He touched no remedies, for he felt them to be useless; he refused the incantations of the medicine-men; alone and in his own strength the war-chief contended with his last enemy.

All over the Willamette Valley, through camp and fishery, ran the whisper that Multnomah was dying; and the hearts of the Indians sunk within them. Beyond the mountains the whisper passed to the allied tribes, once more ripe for revolt, and the news rang among them like a trumpet call; it was of itself a signal for rebellion. The fall of the magic Bridge, the death of Wallulah, and the fatal illness of Multnomah had sealed the doom of the Willamettes. The chiefs stayed their followers only till they knew that he was dead. But the grand old war-chief seemed determined that he would not die. He struggled with disease; he crushed down his sufferings; he fought death with the same silent, indomitable tenacity with which he had overthrown the obstacles of life.

In all his wasting agony he was the war-chief still, and held his subjects in his grip. To the tribes that were about to rebel he sent messages, short, abrupt, but terrible in their threat of vengeance,— messages that shook and awed the chiefs and pushed back invasion. To the last, the great chief overawed the tribes; the generation that had grown up under the 263 shadow of his tyranny, even when they knew he was dying, still obeyed him.

At length, one summer evening a few weeks after the burial of Wallulah, there burst forth from the war-chief's lodge that peculiar wail which was lifted only for the death of one of the royal blood. No need to ask who it was, for only *one* remained of the ancient line that had so long ruled the Willamettes; and for him, the last of his race, was the wail lifted. It was re-echoed by the inmates of the surrounding lodges; it rang, foreboding, mournful, through the encampment on Wappatto Island.

Soon, runners were seen departing in every direction to bear the fatal news throughout the valley. Twilight fell on them; the stars came out; the moon rose and sunk; but the runners sped on, from camp to camp, from village to village. Wherever there was a cluster of Willamette lodges, by forest, river, or sea, the tale was told, the wail was lifted. So all that night the death-wail passed through the valley of the Willamette; and in the morning the trails were thronged with bands of Indians journeying for the last time to the isle of council, to attend the obsequies of their chief, and consult as to the choice of one to take his place.

The pestilence that had so ravaged the household of Multnomah was spread widely now; and every band as it departed from the camp left death behind it,—aye, took death with it; for in each company were those whose haggard, sickly faces told of disease, and in more than one were those so weakened that they lagged behind and fell at last beside the trail to die.

264

The weather was very murky. It was one of the smoky summers of Oregon, like that of the memorable year 1849, when the smoke of wide-spread forest fires hung dense and blinding over Western Oregon for days, and it seemed to the white settlers as if they were never to breathe the clear air or see the sky again. But even that, the historic "smoky time" of the white pioneers, was scarcely equal to the smoky period of more than a century and a half before. The forest fires were raging with unusual fury; Mount Hood was still in course of eruption; and all the valley was wrapped in settled cloud. Through the thick atmosphere the tall firs loomed like spectres, while the far-off roar of flames in the forest and the intermittent sounds of the volcano came weirdly to the Indians as they passed on their mournful way. What wonder that the distant sounds seemed to them wild voices in the air, prophecying woe; and objects in the forest, half seen through the smoke, grotesque forms attending them as they marched! And when the bands had all gathered on the island, the shuddering Indians told of dim and shadowy phantoms that had followed and preceded them all the way; and of gigantic shapes in the likeness of men that had loomed through the smoke, warning them back with outstretched arms. Ominous and unknown cries had come to them through the gloom; and the spirits of the dead had seemed to marshal them on their way, or to oppose their coming,— they knew not which.

So, all day long, troop after troop crossed the river to the island, emerging like shadows from the smoke that seemed to wrap the world,—each with its sickly faces, showing the terrible spread of the pestilence; each helping to swell the great horror that brooded over all, with its tale of the sick and dead at home, and the wild things seen on the way. Band after band the tribes gathered, and when the sun went down the war-chief's obsequies took place.

Multnomah's Death-canoe.

265

It was a strange funeral that they gave Multnomah, yet it was in keeping with the dark, grand life he had lived.

A large canoe was filled with pitch and with pine-knots,—the most inflammable materials an Oregon forest could furnish. Upon them was heaped all that was left of the chief's riches, all the silks and velvets that remained of the cargo of the shipwrecked vessel lost upon the coast long before. And finally, upon the splendid heap of textures, upon the laces and the damasks of the East, was laid the dead body of Multnomah, dressed in buckskin; his moccasins on his feet, his tomahawk and his pipe by his side, as became a chief starting on his last journey.

Then as night came on, and the smoky air darkened into deepest gloom, the canoe was taken out into the main current of the Columbia, and fire was set to the dry knots that made up the funeral pyre. In an instant the contents of the canoe were in a blaze, and it was set adrift in the current. Down the river it floated, lighting the night with leaping flames. On the shore, the assembled tribe watched it in silence, mute, dejected, as they saw their great chief borne from them forever. Promontory and dusky fir, gleaming water and level beach, were brought into startling relief against the background of night, as the burning vessel neared them; then sank into shadow as it passed onward. Overhead, the playing tongues of 266 fire reddened the smoke that hung dense over the water, and made it assume distorted and fantastic shapes, which moved and writhed in the wavering light, and to the Indians seemed spectres of the dead, hovering over the canoe, reaching out their arms to receive the soul of Multnomah.

"It is the dead people come for him," the Willamettes whispered to one another, as they stood upon the bank, watching the canoe drift farther and farther from them, with the wild play of light and shadow over it. Down the river, like some giant torch that was to light the war-chief along the shadowy ways of death, passed the burning canoe. Rounding a wooded point, it blazed a moment brilliantly beside it, and as it drifted to the farther side, outlined the intervening trees with fire, till every branch was clearly relieved against a flaming background; then, passing slowly on beyond the point, the light waned gradually, and at last faded quite away.

And not till then was a sound heard among the silent and impassive throng on the river-bank. But when the burning canoe had vanished utterly, when black and starless night fell again on wood and water, the death-wail burst from the Indians with one impulse and one voice,—a people's cry for its lost chief, a great tribe's lament for the strength and glory that had drifted from it, never to return.

Among a superstitious race, every fact becomes mingled more or less with fable; every occurrence, charged with fantastic meanings. And there sprang up among the Indians, no one could tell how, a prophecy that some night when the Willamettes were 267 in their direst need, a great light would be seen moving on the waters of the Columbia, and the war-chief would come back in a canoe of fire to lead them to victory as of old.

Dire and awful grew their need as the days went on; swift and sweeping was the end. Long did the few survivors of his race watch and wait for his return,—but never more came back Multnomah to his own.

268

CHAPTER V.

AS WAS WRIT IN THE BOOK OF FATE.

A land of old upheaven from the abyss
By fire, to sink into the abyss again,
Where fragments of forgotten peoples dwelt.

TENNYSON.

And now our tale draws to a close. There remains but to tell how the last council was held on Wappatto Island; how Mishlah the Cougar, chief of the Mollalies, died; and how the prophecy of the Bridge was fulfilled.

The morning after the obsequies of Multnomah, the chiefs met in the grove where the great council of the tribes had been held only a few weeks before. The leaves, which had been green and glossy then, were turning yellow and sickly now in the close hot weather. All Nature seemed full of decay.

The chiefs were grouped before the vacant seat of Multnomah; and the Willamette tribe, gathered from canyon and prairie and fishery, looked on, sole spectators of the proceedings,—for none of the allies were present. The ravages of the pestilence had been terrible. Many warriors were missing from the spectators; many chiefs were absent from the council. And there were some present from whom the others shrunk away, whose hot breath and livid faces showed 269 that they too were stricken with the plague. There were emaciated Indians among the audience, whose gaunt forms and hollow eyes told that they had dragged themselves to the council-grove to die. The wailing of the women at the camp, lamenting those just dead; the howling of the medicine-men in the distance, performing their incantations over the sick; the mysterious sounds that came from the burning forest and the volcano,—all these were heard. Round the council the smoke folded thick and dark, veiling the sun, and shutting out the light of heaven and the mercy of the Great Spirit.

The chiefs sat long in silence, each waiting for the other to speak. At length arose a stately warrior famous among the Willamettes for wisdom and prudence.

"We perish," said the chief, "we melt away before the breath of the pestilence, like snow before the breath of the warm spring wind. And while we die of disease in our lodges, war gathers against us beyond the ranges. Even now the bands of our enemies may be descending the mountains, and the tomahawk may smite what the disease has spared. What is to be done? What say the wise chiefs of the Willamettes? Multnomah's seat is empty: shall we choose another war-chief?"

A pale and ghastly chief rose to reply. It was evident that he was in the last extremity of disease.

"Shall we choose another war-chief to sit in Multnomah's place? We may; but will he be Multnomah? The glory of the Willamettes is dead! Talk no more of war, when our war-strength is gone from us. The Bridge is fallen, the Great Spirit is 270 against us. Let those who are to live talk of war. It is time for us to learn how to die."

He sunk flushed and exhausted upon the ground. Then rose an aged chief, so old that it seemed as if a century of time had passed over him. His hair was a dirty gray, his eyes dull and sunken, his face withered. He supported himself with tremulous bony hands upon his staff. His voice was feeble, and seemed like an echo from the long-perished past.

"I am old, the oldest of all the Willamettes. I have seen so many winters that no man can count them. I knew Multnomah's father. I went forth to battle with his father's father; and even before that I knew others, warriors of a forgotten time. Or do I dream? I know not. The weight of the time that I have lived is very heavy, and my mind sinks under it. My form is bowed with the burden of winters. Warriors, I have seen many councils, many troubles, but never a trouble like this. Of what use is your council? Can the words of wise men stay disease? Can the edge of the tomahawk turn back sickness? Can you fight against the Great Spirit? He sent the white man to tell us of our sins and warn us to be better, and you closed your ears and would not listen. Nay, you would have slain him had not the Great Spirit taken him away. These things would not have come upon us had you listened to the white *shaman*. You have offended the Great Spirit, and he has broken the Bridge and sent disease upon us; and all that your wisdom may devise can avail naught to stay his wrath. You can but cover your faces in silence, and die."

For a moment the council was very still. The 271 memory of the white wanderer, his strong and tender eloquence, his fearless denunciation, his loving and passionate appeal, was on them all. *Was* the Great Spirit angry with them because they had rejected him?

"Who talks of dying?" said a fierce warrior, starting to his feet. "Leave that to women and sick men! Shall we stay here to perish while life is yet strong within us? The valley is shadowed with death; the air is disease; an awful sickness wastes the people; our enemies rush in upon us. Shall we then lie down like dogs and wait for death? No. Let us leave this land; let us take our women and children, and fly. Let us seek a new home beyond the Klamath and the Shasta, in the South Land, where the sun is always warm, and the grass is always green, and the cold never comes. The spirits are against us here, and to stay is to perish. Let us seek a new home, where the spirits are not angry; even as our fathers in the time that is far back left their old home in the ice country of the Nootkas and came hither. I have spoken."

His daring words kindled a moment's animation in the despondent audience; then the ceaseless wailing of the women and the panting of the sick chiefs in the council filled the silence, and their hearts sank within them again.

"My brother is brave," said the grave chief who had opened the council, "but are his words wise? Many of our warriors are dead, many are sick, and Multnomah is gone. The Willamettes are weak;

it is bitter to the lips to say it, but it is true. Our enemies are strong. All the tribes who were once with 272 us are against us. The passes are kept by many warriors; and could we fight our way through them to another land, the sickness would go with us. Why fly from the disease here, to die with it in some far-off land?"

"We cannot leave our own land," said a dreamer, or medicine-man. "The Great Spirit gave it to us, the bones of our fathers are in it. It is *our* land," he repeated with touching emphasis. "The Willamette cannot leave his old home, though the world is breaking up all around him. The bones of our people are here. Our brothers lie in the death-huts on *mimaluse* island;—how can we leave them? Here is the place where we must live; here, if death comes, must we die!"

A murmur of assent came from the listeners. It voiced the decision of the council. With stubborn Indian fatalism, they would await the end; fighting the rebels if attacked, and sullenly facing the disease if unmolested. Now a voice was heard that never had been heard in accents of despair,—a voice that was still fierce and warlike in its resentment of the course the council was taking. It was the voice of Mishlah the Cougar, chief of the Mollalies. He, too, had the plague, and had just reached the grove, walking with slow and tottering steps, unlike the Mishlah of other days. But his eyes glittered with all the old ferocity that had given him the name of Cougar. Alas, he was but a dying cougar now.

"Shall we stay here to die?" thundered the wild chief, as he stood leaning on his stick, his sunken eyes sweeping the assembly with a glance of fire. "Shall we stand and tremble till the pestilence slays us all 273 with its arrows, even as a herd of deer, driven into a deep gulch and surrounded, stand till they are shot down by the hunters? Shall we stay in our lodges, and die without lifting a hand? Shall disease burn out the life of our warriors, when they might fall in battle? No! Let us slay the women and children, cross the mountains, and die fighting the rebels! Is it not better to fall in battle like warriors than to perish of disease like dogs?"

The chief looked from face to face, but saw no responsive flash in the eyes that met his own. The settled apathy of despair was on every countenance. Then the medicine-man answered,—

"*You* could never cross the mountains, even if we did this thing. Your breath is hot with disease; the mark of death is on your face; the snake of the pestilence has bitten you. If we went out to battle, you would fall by the wayside to die. Your time is short. To-day you die."

The grim Mollalie met the speaker's glance, and for a moment wavered. He felt within himself that the words were true, that the plague had sapped his life, that his hour was near at hand. Then his hesitation passed, and he lifted his head with scornful defiance.

"So be it! Mishlah accepts his doom. Come, you that were once the warriors of Multnomah, but whose hearts are become the hearts of women; come and learn from a Mollalie how to die!"

Again his glance swept the circle of chiefs as if summoning them to follow him,—then, with weak and staggering footsteps, he left the grove; and it was as if the last hope of the Willamettes went with him. The 274 dense atmosphere of smoke soon shut his form from view. Silence fell on the council. The hearts of the Indians were dead within them. Amid their portentous surroundings,—the appalling signs of the wrath of the Great Spirit,—the fatal apathy which is the curse of their race crept over them.

Then rose the medicine-man, wild priest of a wild and debasing superstition, reverenced as one through whom the dead spoke to the living.

"Break up your council!" he said with fearful look and gesture. "Councils are for those who expect to live! and you!—the dead call you to them. Choose no chief, for who will be left for him to rule? You talk of plans for the future. Would you know what that future will be? I will show you; listen!" He flung up his hand as if imposing silence; and, taken by surprise, they listened eagerly, expecting to hear some supernatural voice or message prophetic of the future. On their strained hearing fell only the labored breathing of the sick chiefs in the council, the ominous muttering of the far-off volcano, and loud and shrill above all the desolate cry of the women wailing their dead.

"You hear it? That death-wail tells all the future holds for you. Before yonder red shadow of a sun"—pointing to the sun, which shone dimly through the smoke—"shall set, the bravest of the Mollalies will be dead. Before the moon wanes to its close, the Willamette race will have passed away. Think you Multnomah's seat is empty? The Pestilence sits in Multnomah's place, and you will all wither in his hot and poisonous breath. Break up your council. Go to your lodges. The sun of the Willamettes is set, 275 and the night is upon us. Our wars are done; our glory is ended. We are but a tale that old men tell around the camp-fire, a handful of red dust gathered from *mimaluse* island,—dust that once was man. Go, you that are as the dead leaves of autumn; go, whirled into everlasting darkness before the wind of the wrath of the Great Spirit!"

He flung out his arms with a wild gesture, as if he held all their lives and threw them forth like dead leaves to be scattered upon the winds. Then he turned away and left the grove. The crowd of warriors who had been looking on broke up and went away, and the chiefs began to leave the council, each muffled in his blanket. The grave and stately sachem who had opened the council tried for a little while to stay the fatal breaking up, but in vain. And when he saw that he could do nothing, he too left the grove, wrapped in stoical pride, sullenly resigned to whatever was to come.

And so the last council ended, in hopeless apathy, in stubborn indecision,—indecision in everything save the recognition that a doom was on them against which it was useless to struggle.

And Mishlah? He returned to his lodge, painted his face as if he were going to battle, and then went out to a grove near the place where the war-dances of the tribe were held. His braves followed him;

others joined them; all watched eagerly, knowing that the end was close at hand, and wondering how he would die.

He laid aside his blanket, exposing his stripped body; and with his eagle plume, in his hair and his stone tomahawk in his hand, began to dance the war-dance 276 of his tribe and to chant the song of the battles he had fought.

At first his utterance was broken and indistinct, his step feeble. But as he went on his voice rang clearer and stronger; his step grew quicker and firmer. Half reciting, half chanting, he continued the wild tale of blood, dancing faster and faster, haranguing louder and louder, until he became a flame of barbaric excitement, until he leaped and whirled in the very madness of raging passion,—the Indian war-frenzy.

But it could not last long. His breath came quick and short; his words grew inarticulate; his eyes gleamed like coals of fire; his feet faltered in the dance. With a final effort he brandished and flung his tomahawk, uttering as he did so a last war-cry, which thrilled all who heard it as of old when he led them in battle. The tomahawk sunk to the head in a neighboring tree, the handle breaking off short with the violence of the shock; and the chief fell back—dead.

Thus passed the soul of the fierce Mollalie. For years afterward, the tomahawk remained where it had sunk in the tree, sole monument of Mishlah. His bones lay unburied beneath, wasted by wind and rain, till there was left only a narrow strip of red earth, with the grass springing rankly around it, to show where the body had been. And the few survivors of the tribe who lingered in the valley were wont to point to the tomahawk imbedded in the tree, and tell the tale of the warrior and how he died.

Why dwell longer on scenes so terrible? Besides, there is but little more to tell. The faithless allies made a raid on the valley; but the shrouding atmosphere 277 of smoke and the frightful rumors they heard of the great plague appalled them, and they retreated. The pestilence protected the Willamettes. The Black Death that the medicine-men saw sitting in Multnomah's place turned back the tide of invasion better than the war-chief himself could have done.

Through the hot months of summer the mortality continued. The valley was swept as with the besom of destruction, and the drama of a people's death was enacted with a thousand variations of horror. When spring came, the invaders entered the valley once more. They found it deserted, with the exception of a few wretched bands, sole survivors of a mighty race. They rode through villages where the decaying mats hung in tatters from the half-bare skeleton-like wigwam poles, where the ashes had been cold for months at the camp-fires; they rode by fisheries where spear and net were rotting beside the canoe upon the beach. And the dead—the dead lay everywhere: in the lodges, beside the fisheries, along the trail where they had been stricken down while trying to escape,—everywhere were the ghastly and repulsive forms.

The spirit of the few survivors was broken, and they made little resistance to the invaders. Mongrel bands from the interior and the coast settled in the valley after the lapse of years; and, mixing with the surviving Willamettes, produced the degenerate race our own pioneers found there at their coming. These hybrids were, within the memory of the white man, overrun and conquered by the Yakimas, who subjugated all the Indians upon Wappatto Island and around the mouth of the Willamette in the early 278 part of the present century. Later on, the Yakimas were driven back by the whites; so that there have been three conquests of the lower Willamette Valley since the fall of the ancient race,—two Indian conquests before the white.

The once musical language of the Willamettes has degenerated into the uncouth Chinook, and the blood of the ancient race flows mixed and debased in the veins of abject and squalid descendants; but the story of the mighty bridge that once spanned the Columbia at the Cascades is still told by the Oregon Indians. Mingled with much of fable, overlaid with myth and superstition, it is nevertheless one of the historic legends of the Columbia, and as such will never be forgotten.

One word more of Cecil Gray, and our tale is done.

The Shoshone renegade, who resolved at Cecil's death to become a Christian, found his way with a few followers to the Flat-Heads, and settled among that tribe. He told them of what he had learned from Cecil,—of the Way of Peace; and the wise men of the tribe pondered his sayings in their hearts. The Shoshone lived and died among them; but from generation to generation the tradition of the white man's God was handed down, till in 1832 four Flat-Heads were sent by the tribe to St. Louis, to ask that teachers be given them to tell them about God.

Every student of history knows how that appeal stirred the heart of the East, and caused the sending out of the first missionaries to Oregon; and from the movement then inaugurated have since sprung all the missions to the Indians of the West.

279

Thus he who gave his life for the Indians, and died seemingly in vain, sowed seed that sprung up and bore a harvest long after his death. And to-day, two centuries since his body was laid in the lonely grave on Wappatto Island, thousands of Indians are the better for his having lived. No true, noble life can be said to have been lived in vain. Defeated and beaten though it may seem to have been, there has gone out from it an influence for the better that has helped in some degree to lighten the great heartache and bitterness of the world. Truth, goodness, and self-sacrifice are never beaten,—no, not by death itself. The example and the influence of such things is deathless, and lives after the individual is gone, flowing on forever in the broad life of humanity.

I write these last lines on Sauvie's Island—the Wappatto of the Indians,—sitting upon the bank of the river, beneath the gnarled and ancient cottonwood that still marks the spot where the old Columbia trail led up from the water to the interior of the island. Stately and beautiful are the far snow-peaks and the sweeping forests. The woods are rich in the colors of an Oregon autumn. The white wappatto blooms along the marshes, its roots ungathered, the dusky hands that once reaped the harvest long crumbled into dust. Blue and majestic in the sunlight flows the Columbia, river of many names,—the Wauna and Wemath of the Indians, the St. Roque of the Spaniards, the Oregon of poetry,—always vast and grand, always flowing placidly to the sea. Steamboats of the present; batteaux of the fur traders; ships, Grey's and Vancouver's, of discovery; Indian 280 canoes of the old unknown time,—the stately river has seen them all come and go, and yet holds its way past forest and promontory, still beautiful and unchanging. Generation after generation, daring hunter, ardent discoverer, silent Indian,—all the shadowy peoples of the past have sailed its waters as we sail them, have lived perplexed and haunted by mystery as we live, have gone out into the Great Darkness with hearts full of wistful doubt and questioning, as we go; and still the river holds its course, bright, beautiful, inscrutable. It stays; *we go.* Is there anything *beyond* the darkness into which generation follows generation and race follows race? Surely there is an after-life, where light and peace shall come to all who, however defeated, have tried to be true and loyal; where the burden shall be lifted and the heartache shall cease; where all the love and hope that slipped away from us here shall be given back to us again, and given back forever.

Via crucis, via lucis.

THE END.

Timeless books such as:

Alice in Wonderland · The Jungle Book · The Wonderful Wizard of Oz
Peter and Wendy · Robin Hood · The Prince and The Pauper
The Railway Children · Treasure Island · A Christmas Carol

Romeo and Juliet · Dracula

Visit
Im TheStory.com
and order yours today!

CPSIA information can be obtained
at www.ICGtesting.com
Printed in the USA
LVOW04s0211151116

512997LV00012B/320/P